the book of abundance

Prosperity Spells, Money Magic and Rituals for a Life
of Wealth and Wellbeing

Cerridwen Greenleaf

Bobby Dazzler Books

Published in 2025 by Jim Dandy Publishing, LLC

6252 Peach Ave
Van Nuys, CA 91411

www.BookThatSaveLives.net

ISBN 13: 978-1-963667-17-2

Printed in the United States

praise for cerridwen greenleaf

"Let the spells in this book work their magic to help you manifest and receive the life of your dreams."

Judika Illes, author of *Encyclopedia of 5,000 Spells*

"While this book suggests that it is all about moon spell magic for love, it covers so much more. With the information in this book, it is the perfect resource for spell casting, rituals as well as deities and flowers. The brief information regarding astrology and the zodiac signs, may spark interest in the area of astrology. Overall, this is a book worth having in your library especially for the resources it provides."

— *Pagan Pages* Magazine

"Moon magic is some of the most powerful of all. What I love about this book is that it has something for everyone, from beginner to advanced wielders of the craft. Cerridwen Greenleaf will help you get your heart's true desire."

Z Budapest, author of *Grandmother Moon*

"Author Cerridwen Greenleaf, can boost many aspects of your life, including romance with techniques for employing moon magic, crystals, and gemstones."

Publisher's Weekly

"Many people scoff at spell books and the idea of magic. However, it's important to note that many people of faith genuinely believe in the practice, and it's not our place to make fun of the religious beliefs and practices of others. Many spell books available for the public are specifically designed for novices and those wanting to dabble for a bit of fun. It's okay to use the book to explore witchcraft. It offers a fun, easy way to engage in the practice without committing. Even if you don't believe magic works, the book offers interesting ideas worth exploring and delicious recipes worth making. It's worth checking out."

Partners in Fire

"Greenleaf is tremendously knowledgeable about these topics and in the way she shares them you feel connected to her. I would say that this is the type of book that those who are open minded and curious about topics connected to meditation and energy sharing. This is definitely a fun read and shows small ways you can try and change your life for the better."

Nerdy Girl Express

contents

Conjuring Prosperity   1
Manifesting a Good Life

1. Money is Energy   3
Learn How to Make It Flow

2. Creating an Abundant Home   12
Feng Shui Secrets

3. Making Money   20
Job-Getting Spells, Luck Charms, and Rituals for Getting a Raise

4. Witch Crafts   24
Candle Cash, Money Bowls, and Prosperous Potions

5. Create a Magical Power Center   38
Your Abundance Altar

6. Planting Prosperity   46
The Rich Witch's Garden

7. Revenue Rocks   59
Lucky Crystals and Stones of Security

Conclusion: Spellcasting a Happy, Healthy, and Wealthy Life   91

Resources   93

About the Author   103

Also by Cerridwen Greenleaf   105

conjuring prosperity
Manifesting a Good Life

I learned very early in life that my fate was mine to guide, and that I could manifest my will through the tools of magic. When in a pinch, I have used witchcraft to replenish the coffers. I have also used prosperity spells to find a good home I could afford to rent, attract job opportunities, and help others in need. People have always marveled at what they perceive as my "good luck," or suggested that I have a fleet of guardian angels behind my every move. But luck has nothing to do with it.

As soon as you approach your prosperity consciously, you will see that you have the power to choose abundance. When you increase your material wealth, you reduce the need to worry about such worldly matters or just getting by day to day. Then, you can move on to achieving true prosperity abundance, expanding your mind through learning, pursuing your pleasures, spending time with family and friends, and enjoying your life.

Witches have always been concerned with real prosperity. Abundance, luck, good fortune, and security are all matters of hearth and home, where good witches preside. The legacy of the pagan approach to prosperity is evident all around if you look with open eyes and ears. It is certainly no accident that paper money has ancient symbols! Every little child knows to look for four-leaf clovers for good luck. These types of "superstitions" are actually common-sense folk wisdom passed down through the centuries.

Every day is an opportunity for growth in every aspect of your life, and the level of your success is entirely up to you. For some, success means a lot of money; for others, success signifies a wealth of real estate; for yet another, success might be making a beautiful painting or sculpture, or a burgeoning garden. Why is this important? Because first, you must know what you want in order to make it manifest. Once you are clear about this, you are on your way to attaining your desires.

money is energy

Learn How to Make It Flow

Phases of the Moon

Performing a spell at optimal times in the lunar cycle will maximize your power. As you read the spells in this book, keep this elemental magic in mind:

Each lunar cycle begins with a "new" phase when the moon lies between the sun and the earth so the illuminated side cannot be seen from earth. The moon gradually "waxes" until it has moved to the opposite side of the earth. When the moon has reached the far side of the earth, its lit side faces us in the "full" moon phase. It then begins to "wane" until it reaches the new moon phase again.

The entire cycle takes a month, during which the moon orbits the earth. To determine the sun sign governing the moon, you will need a celestial guide or almanac. My favorite is Llewellyn's DAILY PLANETARIUM GUIDE. The moon moves from sign to sign every two or three days.

Prompt Prosperity: Money Magic Secrets for True Abundance

For centuries, witches have known that luck is neither random nor mysterious. Thanks to the wise women in my family who share their "trade secrets" openly, I learned very early in life that my fate was mine to guide, and that I could manifest my will through the tools of magic. When in a pinch, I have used witchcraft to replenish the coffers. I have also used prosperity spells to find a good home I could afford to rent, attract job opportunities, and help others. People have always marveled at what they perceive as my "good luck" or suggested that I have a fleet of guardian angels behind my every move, but natural-born good luck has nothing to do with it.

The Manifestor's Mindset: Magical Thinking

I first heard the wisdom of the visionary teacher and writer Louise Hay 25 years ago when my dear friend Duncan gifted me his well-worn cassette tape of her speaking about how to develop a mindset of abundance. I admittedly brought a bit of a scarcity mindset to California with me from West Virginia and was eager to learn new ways. I loved Louise Hay's insights, which were wholly new to me. Duncan patiently explained to me his takeaways from Hay's wisdom and how it had worked for him and changed his life for the better. When paying bills, instead of resenting the utility that had supplied water and electricity, write the check, seal the envelope, and say aloud, "Thank you, Pacific Gas and Electric, for supplying me with power for my home and trusting me to pay you. Blessings to you, PG&E!" We even began a ritual of paying bills together and then walking to the mailbox and pronouncing our gratitude to all the recipients of our money. We even added the finishing touch of kissing the stamped envelopes and saying "Thank you!" before dropping them in for mailing.

We got some looks of surprise at our mailbox rituals, but we believed wholeheartedly in Louise Hay, and doing that had been working for Duncan. Soon, it began to work for me, and I fully embraced the mindset. Most surprising of all, I stopped being filled with dread and worry when bills arrived and started paying them the same day they came in, whenever possible. In addition to adopting an attitude of abundance, it helped my credit score!

In the early 1990s, we had to go to the mailbox for our 5-minute gratitude ritual. Nowadays, with all the instantaneous ways of sending money and electronic payments, it might be closer to a 5-second ritual. However, before you hit "send," get into your Manifestor's Mindset and express thanks before you click or tap. This attitude of abundance that stems from the mindset is like a muscle; the more you use it, the stronger it will be, and you will see many manifestations.

Louise Hay is no longer with us but her brilliance and generosity of spirit remain, and, thanks to all her books and audio, we can still learn from her.

Clearing Your Own Path to Receive Wealth and Happiness

Unless you are already a practitioner of magical arts, you may very well be casting spells unconsciously that throw obstacles in your path. To clear the way to greater wealth and happiness, pick one perfect white rose during the new moon and sit in front of your altar. Light a white candle with your eyes closed. Empty your mind and breathe deeply. When you feel a buzzing at the crown of your head from inhaling and exhaling so mindfully, stare into the flame and repeat seven times:

I am alive.
I have power.
It is real.
I now receive
The flow of plenty
With grace and gratitude.
So mote it be!

Luck By the Cup

When you are crafting money magic, it is good to get in the manifesting mindset with some prosperity tea.

Gather together:

    2 cups fresh water
    Teapot
    Green mug
    Strainer
    1 tablespoon dried rose hips
    1 tablespoon dried chamomile
    1 teaspoon orange peel
    1 cinnamon stick

Steep the rose hips, chamomile, and orange peel in the freshly boiled water for 4 minutes. Strain and pour a cup of tea and stir widdershins, or counterclockwise, in the mug for a moment. As you drink, visualize the abundance coming into your life.

A Spell for Abundant Possibility

I don't know about Thursday's child being "full of woe." I am a Thursday's child and I simply can't relate. Thursday, originally named after the powerful Norse god Thor, is also classically associated with Jupiter, who stands for joviality, expansion, and all things abundant. Here's a Jupiterian spell that will bring excellent opportunities your way.

On a waxing moon Thursday, light one green and one purple candle. Take a sage smudging bundle and put it inside a seashell or fireproof dish. Now, place a concave-shaped rock beside a vase filled with your favorite yellow flowers; dandelions are an excellent choice. Stand in front of your candlelit altar with arms outspread while saying aloud:

As above, so below,
The wisdom of the Mother shall freely flow.
To perfect possibility, I surrender.
So mote it be.

Celebration of Plenty: Morning Meditation

True abundance comes from looking at what you have, rather than focusing on what you lack. This spell is a celebration that will begin each day with magic. Upon waking, take time to reflect on the good things in your life. After meditating upon the blessings in your life, say this spell aloud:

Today and every day,
I see the richness of life.
I thank you, Goddess,
For all the gifts and beauty in my world.
Today, I will share my blessings in others and honor you.
I see plenty for all. Blessings to all
Conclusion: May You Live in Abundance

Binding Prosperity to You: Conjuring Cords

For binding something or someone to you, try this spell during the waxing full moon. To rid yourself of something undesirable, embark on this cord magic during the waning or new moon. Once you have finished, the cords should be given back to the earth by burying them in the ground or tossing them into a body of water, preferably a river. You will need cords or sturdy string in an array of colors. For prosperity, hold a green or gold thread in both hands and envision your desire.

Begin tying knots when you chant:

> *By knot of one, my charms begun,*
> *By two, my charms come true,*
> *By knot of three, my desire is free,*
> *By four, I shall have more,*
> *By knot of five, I will thrive,*
> *By six, ill fortune I nix,*
> *By knot of seven, to Jove in heaven,*
> *So mote it be.*

Most people don't realize that the classic charm bracelet is decorated with magical symbols representing the wearer's wishes. For wealth, wear a Roman coin on your bracelet; for love, try a heart. For protection, a pure silver ring worn on the right pinkie has the greatest magical power, especially when engraved with your birth sign or astrological glyph and sacred pentagram. To instill the ring with protective power, clasp it over your heart and call out:

Into this ring, is safety, security, and the power of
protection.
Guardian energy, be here now!
And so it is.

Lucky Lists!

If prosperity is your real concern, write your wishes on little
paper scrolls and bury them in soil at the foot of a tree. Every
time you water the tree, you will be bringing the wishes closer
to fruition. If luck, happiness, or general goodwill are your
aim, make wishes and hang charms on your tree: colored
ribbons, crystals, anything that strikes your fancy. This should
also be a custom with friends and guests. Every time you add
an ornament, you must also take one down. Only when your
charm has been removed does your wish come true.

Bowl of Plenty

Having an attitude of gratitude lends a sense of satisfaction
and generosity of spirit that will ease your way through the
world. Here's a supremely easy way to give and receive by
acknowledging what you already have:

Take the prettiest and biggest glass bowl, vase, or jar you can
find, and place it on a hallway table or somewhere you pass
every time you enter your house. Light a green candle beside it
and chant:

Pot of gold, full of grace,
Bring good will and gifts to this place.
So mote it be.

Each time you come home, empty your pockets and purse of change. You will be amazed at how quickly the coins multiply. Whenever the vessel fills, take it to the bank and get the coins rolled. Take half and treat yourself to a spirit-raising indulgence; take the other half and give it to your favorite charity, perhaps a homeless shelter or center for battered women. Just like power, generosity of spirit grows and returns to you tenfold. Be prepared for all forms of wealth to come your way.

Abundance Attraction Charm: Almond Anointing Oil

Using almond oil is a simple way to attract money and can be used to ease the discomfort of financial stress. Try rubbing some on your wallet and visualize it filling up with bills. A drop or two on green candles burned every day will make an appreciable difference. Almond oil works quickly because it is ruled by Mercury, the God of speed and communication who operates in the realm of air.

While burning your almond, anointed candles, call upon Mercury:

> *Winged one, bring with you better days.*
> *Blessed be to all and may they*
> *Share in the bounty to come.*
> *With gratitude, blessed be thee!*

Health is Wealth

Throughout your practice, make sure to maintain a sense of personal abundance and acknowledge the great spirit within you. Be grateful for your body and your health. Stand in front of a mirror, preferably naked, and drop all self-criticism.

Chapter One

Concentrate on your real beauty and envelop yourself with unconditional self-love. Wrap your arms around yourself as you say:

In Her/His/Their image, I, too, am a
Goddess/God/Deity.
I walk in beauty; I am surrounded by health, wealth,
and love.
I walk a path of blessings.
And so it is.

creating an abundant home

Feng Shui Secrets

Pagan Feng Shui for Money Magic

I f you want to bring more money into your home or office, place a big chunk of citrine on the left side of your desk, and the money will begin to flow! If you have a dark hallway that feels spooky or an area in your home or office in which the energy feels very static or low, place an obsidian ball there, perhaps on a pedestal, to absorb this negative energy. If you want your bedroom to be a place of bliss and unconditional love, rose quartz will create this all-important atmosphere. Not only will these tips add to the buoyancy and joy of your home, they will also make it more striking and serene.

Place these crystals around your home or workspace for their many benefits:

- Citrine: stronger communication skills
- Lace agate: happiness and joy
- Lapis lazuli: mental brilliance

- Moonstone: self-love and self-expression
- Red coral: good health and physical strength
- Rose quartz or opal: make you appealing to others
- Turquoise: calmness and protection from the earth

Frogs of Fortune

In Japan, the frog presages good fortune. You can keep a little figure of a frog on your desk or wherever you pay bills and manage your personal finances. Your little froggy friend will be a guardian of your income and money.

Sweep Out the Bad Luck and Sweep in the Good

If you or your household had an incident that left behind bad energy, such as a car break-in and theft or suffered from a financial downturn such as a loss of a purse or wallet, it is time to sweep out the bad energy and usher in the prosperous productive energy with your besom, or magical broom. Go to the front door and sprinkle salt on the threshold, then sweep it out of your house. Now sprinkle ground cinnamon, cloves, and nutmeg on your threshold and sweep it into your home. Take a paper towel, scoop up the ground spices, and burn them on your altar in a fireproof dish. All clear now!

Financial Flow: Feng Shui Money Fountain

Ask any feng shui master and they will tell you that water fountains are excellent feng shui and can enhance your prosperity quotient.

Gather together:

A large green bowl or tall vase
Enough water to fill the container
Wooden wand
Small river rocks, at least 8

For those of us who can't pull off a fountain in our home or garden, this works just as well to get the money flowing. Stand in your home's front door area and identify the far-left corner. This is the prosperity area and, therefore, the perfect place for this ritual. Place the smooth river rocks in the bottom of the container and carefully pour the water in, avoiding any spilling. Take up your wand and speak aloud:

In the name of goddess, I dedicate this space.
Peace and prosperity flows throughout this place.
Everyone here will enjoy abundance and grace.
With harm to none. So mote it be.

Take your wand and gently stir the surface of the water so it swirls and circles.

Repeat the spell, then bow and say thank you to abundance energies.

Take the vessel of water and pour it into the roots of the nearest tree, ideally right outside your home or one of your larger potted plants. This will keep the flow of abundance in your personal space.

Speedy Spellcasting: Prosperity Herbs

As a kitchen witch and gardening enthusiast, I am always seeking to learn more about the power of herbs, plants, roots, and flowers that can be used in the craft. Grow your wealth, literally, with these handy money-attraction herbs.

Allspice berries bring good luck; gather seven berries and place them in a small pouch to carry in your pocket or purse for a week. On the seventh day, burn them with cinnamon incense while making your wish for whatever you want.

Basil is a major herb of abundance as well as love. Drop a few fresh basil leaves on the floor of your kitchen and sweep them out of your home with your magical broom while speaking this charm: *"Scarcity is out the door; no longer will I be poor. Health and wealth, be here now. Harm to none, so mote it be."*

Cinnamon has come to be called the "Sweet Money Spice" as this delightfully scented herb brings luck and will make a business more prosperous. Sprinkle a dash of powdered cinnamon on the threshold of your front door, store, or business, and watch the wealth walk in!

Cloves are herbs of good fortune and even help in gambling. They also bring people together and bind them. If you need to turn your luck around, use cloves in spell work as an herbal element or in incense or potpourri to foment abundant energy.

Ginger root can speed up any magic. You can grind up the dried ginger root into powder and add to your money attraction spells, bringing the funds much sooner. Ginger tea brings money your way, briskly!

Nutmeg is another spice beloved by gamesmen and gamblers. Carry a whole nutmeg in your pocket and your luck will improve the same day.

Thyme is a common herb that will attract money to your home. Every time you cook with it you draw abundance and wealth toward you. Drink thyme tea for a quick fortune turnaround and fast money magic with this spell: "*It is time for money to come my way; good luck is mine. Money thyme is mine with blessings for all.*"

Plan Your Week with Color Craft

Candle magic is a mainstay of witchcraft. I burn candles every night and also take them with me when traveling. For their magic to work, simply apply the basic precepts of color magic: have a clear intention of your desired outcome, and choose the appropriate color candle from the following list. On the corresponding day, begin burning the candle on your altar. Repeat this ritual for seven consecutive days with the same color candle. If you're traveling, choose a spot to consecrate as an altar using the prosperity altar incantation at the beginning of this chapter.

Sunday

The Sun rules this day; use gold or red to affect a boss, a promotion, health, fame, or success.

Monday

The moon rules this day; use silver or orange to affect home, subordinates, or the emotions.

Tuesday

Planet Mars rules; yellow is the color that affects aggression, sex, conflict, and confidence.

Wednesday

Mercury rules; green is the color that affects communication, study, and quicker intelligence.

Thursday

Jupiter rules; the color blue affects medical and legal issues, money, spirit, integrity, safety, and security.

Friday

Venus rules; use indigo to affect aesthetics and beauty, marriage, relationships, theater, art, music, and family.

Saturday

Saturn rules; black is the color affecting judgment, obstacles, or property.

Crystal Feng Shui for Luck and Happiness

Place these objects in your home to attract loving energy like new friends and relationships:

- Two crystals of rose quartz of equivalent size,
- Pink, orange, or red fabric,
- Two red candles, and
- Images of two butterflies.

Maple Tree Magic - Prosperity Rite

As always, you can create your own luck and stimulate the

flow of money into your life with this ever-so-helpful tree energy and the special magic of maple.

You will need:

- A green stone like Aventurine and Red sardonyx
- Silver or gold coins (i.e., new pennies/nickels/quarters/dimes/silver dollars or Feng Shui Chinese Coins)
- Lodestone Magnetic sand in silver or gold (available online)
- Money drawing potion (mix 3 teaspoons ground maple leaves together with 3 teaspoons sugar)
- A small purple bowl

Directions:

1. Place the coins in the bowl.
2. Place the stones on top of the coins.
3. Sprinkle 1/3 of the money drawing potion and 4 tablespoons of the magnetic sand over the coins and the stones.
4. Place the bowl under your bed and be sure no pets or children can get into the bowl. Say: *"Prosperity finds me and blesses me with its bounty, this day and every day, Amen."* (Or however you close a prayer or affirmation.)
5. Every 3 days for a total of 3 times, sprinkle the bowl with another third of the money drawing potion and 1 more tablespoon of magnetic sand.
6. Each night before going to sleep, hold the bowl in your hands and visualize how prosperity will find you, how you feel when you have it, and exactly what you can do to attract it. Be very specific ("I

will do x, y, and z to bring prosperity into my life"). Hold this thought in your mind as you place the bowl back under your bed and go to sleep.

7. After nine days, accept that the prosperity spell is complete. Return the ingredients to the earth (you may keep the stone and coins with you) and know that Prosperity is yours.

8. Make a list of all the things that you already have that make you feel prosperous. Bless them and leave the list under the stone and coins. Read the list daily.

making money

Job-Getting Spells, Luck Charms, and Rituals for Getting a Raise

You can make your own luck; that is the purpose of magic. Money magic is the most practical kind of magic, too. Manifesting more personal wealth is not selfish at all as it means you will be better able to be more part of your community, make contributions, and also, by reducing the stress of living with a sense of lack, you can be more creative, more productive, and bring more love, abundance, and joy to your loved ones. Isn't that what life is all about?

GO FORTH AND MANIFEST!

Change-Your-Luck Rite

Perhaps you have been overwhelmed recently by a series of unfortunate events – problems with work, finances, etc.– seemingly beyond your control. Do away with these burdens as quickly as possible. This spell requires paper, a black candle, a flat rock with a hollow in the center to set the candle into, a black ink pen, and a "cancellation" stamp, readily available at any stationary store. Anoint your candle with a drop of peppermint oil. Dress your altar with a peony blossom, the luckiest of the flower family. The consummate time to release bad luck is immediately after the full moon. Write what you wish to be freed from on a piece of parchment or stationery; this is your "release request." Write this same request onto the candle as well. Ideally, this is scratched into the candle with the thorn of a rose you have grown yourself. Light the candle near an open window so the negative energy will leave your home.

While the candle burns, intone:

Waxing moon, moist wise Cybele, from me this burden please dispel. Upon this night so clear and bright I release _____ to the moon tonight.

Burn the candle for thirteen minutes. Take your stamp and mark the paper "canceled." Put the candle out, fold the paper away from you, and place it under the candle stone. Repeat this process for thirteen nights. On the last night, which should be the beginning of the new moon phase, burn the paper and bury the candle, paper ashes, and rock far from your home. Give thanks to the moon for assisting you, and let go of the bad luck.

Employment Incantation

Here is one way I got a great job on my first day in San Francisco, despite the fact that I wasn't really qualified, and I looked like an absolute hayseed after driving cross-country for four straight days from Appalachia.

Light a gold candle, although red will also do. Repeat this

incantation eight times while holding a vision of yourself at the desired job:

I see the perfect job for me;
I see a place of plenty. Upon my heart's desire,
I am set; My new boss will never regret.
This job will come to me NOW.
Harm to none I VOW.
So mote it be.

Money Blessings Bath

Before you go to your job interview, slip into a magic money bath! This spell is most effective if practiced on a new or full moon Thursday night. Pour green apple or mint essential oil into running bath water and bathe by the light of a single green candle. As you close your eyes, meditate on your true desires. What does personal prosperity mean to you? What do you really need and what do you really want? When you are clear about your answers, focus on the candle flame while whispering:

Here and now,
My intention is set.
New luck will be mine.
All needs will be met.
With harm to none and plenty for all.
Blessed be.

Your Personal Pot of Gold

Cauldron magic is less about the eye of a newt than it is about purification by water and pungently perfumed herbs. For a money-attraction brew, fill a big pot with fresh water and place it on your altar during the waxing moon. Place an offering bowl nearby filled with a tablespoon of honey mixed into a cup of milk. Toss a dry palmful of chamomile, woodruff, moss, and vervain into the cauldron.

Head uplifted, utter:

I call upon you, Gods and Goddesses of old,
To fill my purse with gold.
In return, I offer you honey's gold and mother's milk.
With harm to none and blessings to thee,
I honor you for bringing me health and prosperity.

Place the bowl outside as your offering and leave it overnight. Whatever the ancients have left behind, pour it into the ground and bow in gratitude for the generosity of the Gods towards you.

Tips 'n' Tricks: Falling Leaves

Here's a sweet bit of alchemy available to all, handed down from medieval times. Wise women of old taught their children to watch for falling leaves. To catch one in midair is the best kind of luck, direct from Mother Earth herself. Carry it with you for a season and you will be kept safe from harm and receive unseen rewards. If you are especially blessed and catch more than one falling leaf, share it with the one closest to you. You will be bound by both love and fortune.

four
witch crafts

Candle Cash, Money Bowls, and
Prosperous Potions

From time immemorial, witches have been very crafty. Hedge witches and healing women from ancient times were extremely resourceful because they had to be; they needed to take care of their families and oftentimes their community. They mastered the art of growing and foraging for the bounty of the fields and forests, searching for herbs and roots for medicine and food for feeding the tribe. This same resourcefulness gave our pagan elders an advantage with crafting as they were thrifty and good at figuring out how to repurpose and get the most possible use out of whatever they had. Those same traits and talents have been passed down to us; crafty witches avail today and you can often find their wares at metaphysical bookstores, apothecaries, and so many other retailers including Etsy. When I was a little girl growing up on a farm, my aunts seemingly knew every craft—they were such gifted and creative women! Aunt Ida made doilies that the Etsy crowd would covet while her sister, Ivy, tatted the most perfect lace; it was stunningly beautiful.

I was taught how to sew, quilt, and crochet by my mother, Helen, and her sister, Aunt Ruth, who was a fantastic cook and gardener. As soon as I could toddle behind her in the garden, I learned how to plant flowers and veggies, and I was quite proud of myself that I knew how to propagate new plants from starts as well as graft. If you ever take a drive with me in the countryside, be prepared to stop often so we can get clippings for starters from what might be growing at the side of the road, using the kit I keep in the trunk of my old hybrid (don't worry, we will be careful to pull as far off as possible and you'll be quite safe). I have a few prized fruit trees that didn't cost a penny, coming from the bounty of the goddess.

My mom's best friend, Marilyn, had a loom in her living room that was used daily by both her and her mother, who had the unforgettable and charming name Dixie. Any old towels, socks, any and all garments, and even tea towels that were judged to be past their prime got ripped into small pieces by this clever duo and got turned into rag rugs. While the name was humble and homely, the rugs they crafted were not. They were wonderfully colorful, felt good under your toes, and brightened any room. We brought worn-out fabric over to their house and feasted on tea cake while rugs were produced during our visit. Their production crafting became so popular that they started selling them from their home at a fast clip. I have one of Marilyn and Dixie's eye-catching works of art at my kitchen sink. Every time I see it, I think of how these women gathered in friendship and through their pure ingenuity, spun old rags into gold.

I was lucky indeed to grow up on a farm surrounded by relatives and friends who were very crafty women.

Wand Crafting: DIY Manifestation Tool

Gather together:

A found piece of wood
Sandpaper
Copper wire (12 inches in length)
A large pebble-sized crystal

If you find the perfect piece of wood, sand it to smoothness so it feels good in your hand, which is very important. If your found wood branch is too long, use your chosen magical knife to cut it down to 12 inches or your preferred length. Wrap copper wire around the top and affix the crystal of your preference to the end. Your wand should look beautiful to your eye so embellish it with ornaments you love such as beads, sequins, seashells, tiny crystals, or whatever pleases your eye and adds to the power of this sacred implement.

Pointing to Prosperity to Boost Your Blessings

If your wand can fit well on your altar, I suggest keeping it there. You can also use the crystal at the end to boost the power of any rituals you are working on your altar. For example, whatever ritual elements symbolize money, health or love, point the wand at those for an extra charge of positive wealth energy.

Money Bags

Rather than chasing money or possessions, a wise witch will simply draw them to her. A tiny green pouch filled with the herb vervain, for positive change in your life, is a powerful tool for attracting all nature of good fortune.

Prepare your attraction pouch during the waxing moon (ideally in Taurus). Hold it over frankincense incense and let the smoke bless the bag as you speak aloud:

The moon is a golden coin, Cybele.
I carry your abundance with me.
Blessing upon thee and me.

Herbal Wreaths Make a Home

Oftentimes, your kitchen is the heart of the home. Something about cooking and sharing food brings people together. An herbal wreath hanging on the kitchen door can be a source of love and luck. You'll need the following for your creation:

- Freshly cut herbs of your choice
- A wire wreath frame, available from most craft stores
- Either string or florist's wire, ribbon, and a hot glue gun

This is truly one of the simplest craft projects you can ever make–simply use the wreath frame as a base, and use string or the florist's wire to anchor the fresh herbs into place. Finish it off with a colorful ribbon or other magical decorative touches you may want to add.

Curative Wreath: These are the ideal herbs for a wreath that brings curative properties including lavender, barley, comfrey, rosemary peppermint, borage, olive, eucalyptus, and apple blossom. Brown and green ribbons add a touch of healing color.

Security Wreath: Hang this guardian wreath on your front door using heather, holly, dill, foxglove, garlic, sandalwood, snapdragon, mustard, foxglove, mistletoe, and mugwort. White and blue ribbons add security and serenity.

Prosperity Wreath: Greet prosperity at the door with herbs associated with money magic, which include clover, chamomile, sunflower, apple, cinnamon, myrtle, basil, and bay leaf. Weave in gold and green ribbon to add to your luck.

Growing Riches: Reaping What You Sow

The San Francisco Bay Area is magical in spring and summer, with its profusion of poppies growing along the highway and in every available crevice. No wonder California is one of the wealthiest places in the world: Pagans revere poppies for their money magic. If you have a yard, meadow, or any strip of ground you can garden, buy poppy seeds and simply toss them all around. Two months later, you will have a wealth of wildflowers.

Harvest the dried seed pods and store some for replanting next winter. Place the rest in a tiny green to gold cloth bag.
Bless the bag with these words:

> *Poppy, gold like the sun, thank you for the new luck I've won.*

Sow the seed bag shut and carry it in your pocket, purse, or wallet.

Envisioning Your Prosperous Future: DIY Visionary Incense

You can access your prophetic capabilities with a Wednesday incense ritual using:

3 palmfuls ground chicory root
1 palmful ground cloves
3 palmfuls cinquefoil*

*Cinquefoil is in the dandelion family. If you can't find any, use dandelion roots and stems.

Mix and burn the herbs in your fireplace or on your altar while concentrating on a question like whether to take a new job or pursue a business venture. Use this time to cleanse your mind of all concerns, worries, and thoughts, making way for pure insight. Answers will come.

Power Wand

Prosperity and purification go hand in hand. One of the greatest tools for purification, sage, can be found growing wild by most roadsides and in many meadows. While every meta-physical store has it in quantity, I highly recommend growing and harvesting it yourself. Aromatic sage dries quickly and can effortlessly be bound into thick "smudge sticks" which you should keep at the ready in a fireproof clay dish.

To make a smudge stick, take dried sage leaves and bind them with green and gold thread, wound nine times around the bundles, and knot at each loop. Leave room for a "handle" at the base of the wand.

Knot the green and gold threads thrice more. This will honor the muses and please the fates that hold the thread of all our lives in their hands.

Use your smudge stick any time a purification is in order, especially if you've moved, started a new job, bought a new car, or purchased any "recycled" clothing or furniture. This will help remove any energy that might be clinging from the previous owner.

Light your smudge stick and, moving clockwise, circle the areas or items to be purified.

Speak aloud:

Great spirit, with this smoke, your blessed protection I invoke. Out with the bad, in with the good. With harm to none.

Witch Craft; DIY Luck Eternal Amulets

Rarely will you see an unjeweled pagan, as they usually wear at least a single ring or pendant, and know full well that jewelry can be used as defense!

Witches know the meaning, power, and properties of each stone and metal and wield that energy for the good of others and themselves. The term *amulet* comes from the Latin word meaning "defense." Indeed, amulets are a way to protect yourself that dates from the earliest human beliefs. Evil eyes might be the most global of all amulets, as they are believed to ward off a hex by simply reflecting it back to its origins. Some amulets were devoted to a specific god or goddess, offering that deity's sheltering protection.

You can make a powerful protective amulet with only two items: a tiny muslin pouch and a tablespoonful of dried herbs. The following is a list of herbs from which to choose for the specific kind of safeguard you feel you need. Amulets are very easy to create and make nice gifts, as long as you feel your friend will truly benefit from and is aware of the special qualities and power of such. It can also be a small gift to yourself that yields big benefit. Wear your amulet as a pendant or tuck it in your pocket or purse for a "guardian to go."

- **Spanish Moss** can banish poltergeists and absorb curses, hexes, and black magic.
- **Dandelion** provides shielding energy and also clears away the negative.

- **Marigold** helps you communicate with the spirit world and those who passed on.
- **Burdock Root** keeps travels safe and also protects you from anger and jealousy,
- **Clover** will guard against misfortune and invite good faeries into your life.
- **Asphodel** rids your home of unwanted energies and sends a ghost on its way to the afterlife.
- **Betony** keeps sleep disturbances at bay and forestalls nightmares for deep sleep.
- **Agrimony** is a defensive herb used to banish evil spirits and repels hostile magic.
- **High John the Conqueror** banishes bad magic and brings good luck to you

A Pocket Full of Luck: The Advantage of Amulets

For an optimal outcome to any important meeting–whether business or social–take an amulet with you. It can be a tiny sack hidden in a pocket or contained in a locket. Fill your amulet with any of the following herbs:

For courage, try **borage** or **mullein.**

To avoid betrayal, **snapdragon** will serve you well.

For robust health, **rue** will do the trick.

To overcome nervousness, a mixture of **dried yarrow and nettle** is potent.

To identify another witch, **ivy, rue, broom straw, agrimony, and fern** work best.

For travel, always wear **comfrey** for safety.

For youthful energy, the **oak's acorn** will vitalize you.

For strength and physical stamina, tuck some **mugwort** in your shoes.

To ensure victory, **woodruff** assures a winner.

To guarantee a friendly exchange, **heliotrope** will make for good conversation.

Coin Conjuration

We all have unexpected expenses that come out of the blue–car repairs, medical bills, or helping a loved one in need. I had the latter with my family and had to reach deep into my coffers to heed the call. When you need to quickly recover financially, this coin spell will fill the bill, literally.

Gather together:

- 13 coins of different denominations
- Athame
- A green or gold jar with a lid
- 3 gold or yellow candles
- 3 yellow or gold-colored crystals such as tiger's eye, amber, citrine, yellow jade, or another favorite of yours
- Frankincense or myrrh incense
- 3 pieces of golden fruit such as yellow apples, oranges, or other yellow or gold-colored fruit

On the evening of a new moon or a waxing moon phase when the moon is increasing, make a quick temporary altar where you pay your bills and handle your money–maybe it is your desk or perhaps, the kitchen table. Use your athame to create the circle of magic at this soon-to-be sacred space. Place the candles, incense, crystals, and fruit there and arrange them so a crystal, apple, and candle are each in a group. Light your candles and the incense. Take the coins in your hands and pass over the incense smoke. Place the coins in the jar. Now take the crystals in your hand and pass through the smoke, then place in the jar and seal. Pick up one piece of fruit at a time and touch to your third eye (in the middle of your forehead).

Pray aloud:

> *This offering I make as my blessing to all,*
> *Comfort and earthly gifts upon us shall fall.*
> *Fill my coffers with silver and gold.*
> *In this time of great need, I will be bold.*
> *For the good of all, young and old.*
> *Fill my coffers with silver and gold.*
> *And so it is.*

Extinguish the candles and incense and place on your altar for future use as well as the vessel containing the coins. When you go to sleep, dream of everyone you love, including yourself, receiving a harvest of material and spiritual wealth.

Blissful Blend: Basil Infusion Oil

Infusions have regained popularity as a way of getting as much of the herb into oil as possible, it is a method that brings the flavors of one food, in this case, fresh herbs, to another, such as oil. Basic Oil is unbelievably easy to make. You'll need:

> 2 ounces fresh basil
> 3/4 cups virgin olive oil (you can use safflower oil or canola)

Ideally, you gather your fresh herbs in your own kitchen garden but any farmer's market or organic grocery will have green herbs. For the best and purest flavor, use fresh herbs at their peak. Rinse thoroughly in cold water. Gently pat dry with paper towels and give the basil a coarse chop. Place into a metal colander and dip into boiling water for 10 seconds. Rinse in an ice water bath and drain well. Gently pat dry and add the basil to the oil. After three to five days in a cool dark place, the flavor will have infused into the oil, adding the fresh bright green note of the herbs. Use liberally on roasts, salads, drizzling on top of cooked vegetables and soups. Basil not only confers much palatability but it also brings prosperity. Enjoy!

These herbs also make fantastic infused oils: rosemary. tarragon, parsley, chives, and cilantro.

Pantry Power – Plant Infusions for An Abundant Life

Many enthusiasts enjoy several cups a day of their favorite herbal infusion which is a large portion of herb brewed for at least four hours and as long as ten. I recommend placing one cup of the dried herb into a quart canning jar and filling it with freshly boiled water. After the steeping, strain with a non-metallic method such as cheesecloth or bamboo. Herbal infusions can be made with the leaves and fruits which provide healing aspects of this comforting brew. Many of the favorite kitchen garden herbs contain minerals, antioxidants, and phytochemicals including the list herein.

What do you need to attend to in your life now? This list of herbs and associations can be your guide; one of the smartest ways to approach this methodology is to brew right before bedtime and you will awaken to a freshly infused herb. Some of the most popular herbs and fruits used to create infusions are as follows:

- **Caraway Seeds** aid in relationships
- **Catnip Leaves** make women even more attractive
- **Chamomile Flowers** help with sleep, good for abundance
- **Dandelion Leaves** make wishes come true
- **Echinacea** makes the body strong
- **Nettle Leaves** will break any hex
- **Pine Needles** increase skin health as well as financial health
- **Sage Leaves** purify energy, act as an antibiotic
- **St. John's Wort** is an antidepressant that lifts spirits
- **Thyme Leaves** are a protectant for you and your property
- **Yarrow Flowers** reduce fever, bring courage and good luck

Spirit Soothing Massage Candles

Making massage candles is very similar to making any other type of potted candle. I recommend using soy wax as it is super gentle on the skin. Soy wax is also nice and soft so it melts easily and stays together in a puddle after melting, and can be reused for us thrifty crafters. If you have a soy allergy, you can use the ever-so-popular beeswax instead (for example, it is in nearly every single Burt's Bees product). Essential oils or cosmetic-grade fragrance oils are also added to create a soothing atmosphere. All soap-making fragrances that are also soy candle-safe are perfect choices for scenting your massage candles. Try the basic directions below to make your first candle. For every three ounces of wax, you'll add one ounce of liquid oil and one-quarter ounce of fragrance. I suggest making two candles in four-ounce metal tins while you master this craft.

Gather together:

> 2 ounces sweet almond carrier oil or vitamin E oil
> 6 ounces high quality soy wax
> Half an ounce essential oil
> 2 4-ounce metal tins
> 2 6-inch candle wicks
> Double boiler pan with water

Directions:

1. Melt the soy wax and oil in a double boiler over simmering water.
2. Add the essential oils and stir gently to avoid bubbling or spilling,
3. Once the wax has cooled somewhat but is still melted enough to pour, place the wicks in your containers and pour the wax.
4. Allow several hours for the candles to set and harden
5. Trim the wicks to one-quarter of an inch above the top of the candle, and they're ready to use.

Easy Money Homemade Incense

As you may have noticed from your reading, I treasure cinnamon incense. It brings a positive energy to your space with its appealingly sweet and spicy scent. It also brings prosperity and calm. What could be better? This may become one of your favorites, as well as it is truly easy to make.

Gather together:

1 tablespoon ground cinnamon
1 teaspoon of water
Small bowl
Baking sheet
Small glass votive container

Spoon the powdered cinnamon into the middle of your bowl
and mix in the water well. When the consistency is close to
that of damp sand, you are good. Using your hands, knead the
mixture into your desired shape which could be a cone, pyra-
mid, ball, or even a heart. Place this onto your baking sheet
and bake at 325 degrees for 15 minutes. Pull it out of the oven
and let it cool. Once your incense creation is at room tempera-
ture, place it in the glass votive for when you want to use it.
These DIY incenses take a few seconds to light but their capti-
vating scents are so worth it.

DIY Enchanted Incenses:

- **Ginger** will bring more money into your space as well as success.
- **Cardamom** is used in love magic and will also bring you tranquility.
- **Allspice** is quite effective in healing work.
- **Nutmeg** awakens psychism and prophetic dreams.
- **Clove** is excellent in protection and banishing.

five
create a magical power center
Your Abundance Altar

Your altar is the nexus of your magical powers; it is also your medium through which you give gifts to the Roman god of abundance, Jupiter, also known as Jove. Jupiter is a rain and thunder deity who also controls fertility. He will rain abundance down upon you if you gain his favor through ritual observance. His "jovial" qualities include leadership, jollity, generosity, expansiveness, and a royal manner. Your middle finger is your Jupiter finger and you can increase your fortunes by leaving a ring on your altar overnight and then placing it upon the middle finger of either hand. Ideally, for the best result, it will be a green or gold stone such as peridot, tourmaline, or citrine. If you can find a statue or bust of Jove, you should place this symbol on the right side of the altar, accompanied by the image of an eagle, which is the ideal prosperity altar emblem, as the eagle is Jupiter's bird totem. The eagles of Rome and America are this royal bird of the king of gods. Lapis lazuli, the beautiful blue stone beloved by the Egyptians, is also sacred to Jupiter. The alchemical symbol for this stone is the astrological sign of Jupiter in reverse, and the blue of the Lapis stone is associated with the blue of the sky god. You can increase your prosperity by remembering one of the most basic principles of prosperity: *By giving, so shall you receive.*

Your Abundance Altar

An important first step to money magic is to make an area in your home that is dedicated to abundance. To create a prosperity altar, cover a low table with green and gold scarves; then select a candle to match. Each day "recharge" the blessings with an altar gift, such as flowers, quartz crystals, gorgeously scented amber resin, or coin-shaped pebbles.

On the new moon, light your candles at midnight and burn frankincense and myrrh incense. Make an offering of tiger eye or citrine crystals, a golden apple or a peach, and anoint your third eye (in the middle of your forehead) with a corresponding essential oil – myrrh or frankincense, apple or peach.

Pray aloud:

> *This offering I make as my blessing to all,*
> *Comfort and earthly gifts upon us shall fall.*
> *Blessed be.*

Let the candles burn all night and dream of everyone you love, including yourself, receiving a harvest of material and spiritual wealth

The Good Life Altar

To prepare the way for letting new opportunities enter your life or to focus your attention on existing friendships, set up an altar where you can concentrate your energy and clarify your intentions. If you already have an altar in place, incorporate some of the following elements to enhance your relationships with others as well as with yourself. The more you use your altar, the more powerful your spells will be.

Your altar can be a low table, the top of a shelf, or even the shelf itself. First, purify the space with the smoke of a lit sage bundle. This is called "smudging" and is an essential part of witchcraft. You can use wild sage or purchase it in any herb store. Once you have smudged the space, cover your altar with a pink-colored scarf or cloth, and place pink and white candles in each of the four corners (Pink is the color of affection and White represents purity intention). Place rose quartz and calming fluorite stones around a vase of fresh flowers often with poppies, daisies, whatever connotes fun and friendship to you.

As a centerpiece, place on the altar a photograph of your friends or an image that represents abundance for you in your life.

Light the candles, kneel before your newly created altar, and say:

> *I light the fire of loyalty*
> *The heat of heart and the flame of friendship.*
> *Brightest blessing, Great Goddess bring,*
> *The spirit of friendship will surely sing.*
> *As the fates do dance, I welcome the chance*
> *To share my love and my life.*
> *So mote it be.*

Wands of Wonder: A Magic Money Tool

A wand is used for directing energy. It is best to make your wand from found wood and instill it with your personal energy. You can go out into a nearby park or the woods to find a suitable branch that has fallen. Never cut a wand from a tree, as that energy will be retained by the wand. Allow Mother Nature to choose one for you; she is always right. You might find the perfect weathered wand on a beach as driftwood. Each tree has its distinctive properties:

Ash: Ash grows fast, and its seedlings root everywhere, so it's persistent. Use ash for prosperity, transformation, and self-improvement.

Birch: Use a birch wand for healing spells, for calming situations, and for requesting a diplomatic solution or a good outcome for any business meeting.

Crab Apple: will provide bent and twisted, gnarled wands. Apple, as we know, is the tree of knowledge and wisdom and also represents plenty. They are wonderful tools for guidance.

Rowan or Mountain Ash: This is a "portal tree", therefore when you want to undertake a journey or a guided visualization, keep your Mountain Ash wand close by.

Oak: is also good for healing and protection. It makes a good, long-lasting wand for intensely focused work. If you choose to use only one wand, make it oak.

Set Your Money Intention

Adorn your altar with fresh flowers and three candles in your favorite shade of green. Also, gather a pen and paper. Light the candles and sit in front of your altar while you meditate on what will make you achieve your full potential.

Do you need to change your money habits? Your approach to spending and finances? Do you need to open your creativity? Do you need to revitalize with a vacation?

Concentrate deeply, and choose three intentions for positive change in your life to write down and place under your three candles.

Every night for seven days, repeat this spell:

> *Today I arise. This day I embrace serenity and money wisdom.*
> *Tonight, I rest. This night I embrace an attitude of abundance and calm.*
> *Blessed be.*

Your Week of Witchy Wealth

Each day of the week holds special meaning that can impact your prosperity.

Sunday

Is the day of our greatest star, Sol, otherwise known as the Sun, with colors of gold, orange, and radiant white. This is the time to rest and renew, indulge in creativity, and enjoy the fruits of this life. Sunday is the time to strike for fame and fortune. Make yourself heard.

Monday

Comes from the moon day and is ruled by the moon goddess known variously as Diana, Cybele, Artemis, and Selene. It is associated with all the hues of blue from sapphire to pearly iridescent. This is the day for divination, deep reflection, and love, especially loving your true nature. Tap into your intuition to know how you can improve your finances. Make notes!

Tuesday

Named for Tiw's day, is ruled by Mars, the God of war and action. This day wears the colors red and pink. Like the old saying, "Tuesday is good news day," this day is auspicious for matters regarding prosperity, truth, new beginnings, and high energy with focus. Good day for new projects.

Wednesday

Comes from Woden's day and is associated with the winged God of communication, Mercury, whose color is yellow. This is the day for interaction and initiation, presenting a good opportunity for this fourth day. Also sacred to the Yoruban Goddess Oshun and is associated with water energy and flowing.

Thursday

Thursday stands for strength, joy, performance, extravagance, and great staying power. It is an optimal time to try something new or make a new contact for new business. Excellent time for a new deal.

Friday

Known as Freya's Day, it is Venusian in nature. Its color, green, is associated with fertility, love, nature, abundance, and joy-filled sex. This is a good day to ask for a raise.

Saturday

Associated with black and gray, it is the day of the ruling judge Saturn. This is when we must take stock of the week, get errands and personal business done, and finish the day off with a ritual meal with friends and loved ones. Celebrate abundance and count your blessings, which creates more goodness.

Flowers of Fortune Altar Enchantment

The more you tend your altar, the more of your personal magic is inculcated in that sacred space. In regard to the great magical undertaking of your well-being, it is vital that you imbue your altar with your essence and your energy. For this enchantment, start at noon on Sunday and repeat through Saturday.

Gather together:

Photo of you
Small pedestal
Favorite piece of birthstone jewelry
Vase filled with fresh water
4 of any of the following flowers: yellow daisy, yellow rose, sunflower, or lily

Take a photo of yourself that you love, one that represents you looking both healthful and joyful. Add symbols that represent you: a favorite ring or other jewelry, ideally, with your birthstone, Take the photos and symbol and place it on a pedestal on your altar. In front of the pedestal, place a small vase with four Flowers of Fortune. These posies will bring you abundance which includes both wealth and health. The yellow signifies the vigor and sun-blessed energy that will increase your strength and vivacity every time you speak the following spell:

*On this earth and under these stars, I call upon the Gods
to bring great help and good fortune to me, _____
(your name).*

Place the beloved piece of jewelry on

*In this air and through these waters, speed fortune here
in my name of _____.*

Now touch the stone in the ring.

*Through the fire and through the rain, bring me glad-
ness, goodwill, and great health!
To me here and now.*

Remove the jewelry, place it back on your altar, and repeat the
next day at noon. Each day, you should awaken feeling cheerier
and more content.

planting prosperity

The Rich Witch's Garden

Our wise elders from hundreds of years ago knew this very well: herbs, flowers, and many plants, trees, and vegetables bring abundance into your life. They utilized this knowledge to the benefit of their communities and were forward-thinking; many a garden, grove of trees, vineyard, and orchard were planted by our forebears who wanted to provide for their children's children and future generations. Not only were they ensuring their communities would enjoy the bounty of plentiful fruit, nuts, grapes, and berries, but they were also leaving behind a legacy of beauty and prosperity.

I also had the great fortune to grow up in the countryside on a farm. Much of what I know I learned from my wise aunt about herbs to gather in the wild, like which foods to cook for love, money, luck, health, and in celebration of the high holidays. It is exciting to go to the garden, the grocery store, or the farmer's market and bring home the ingredients for positive life change. In addition to the secrets to magical cooking, I learned from this wise woman that the first task to undertake is to clean your kitchen and purify it. If anything needs repairing, fix it. Any utensils, pots, or pans that are banged up can be donated. If your kitchen curtains look shabby to your eye, make or buy new ones. If there is a bag of rice or beans past the prime, compost away. You should clean the cooking space in both the practical sense and also to cleanse it in the magical sense. Health is wealth, really and truly. Prepare your kitchen and altar to be used for the purpose of prosperity,

Prosperous Plantings

Flower essences that can enhance prosperity include:

- **Carnation** or **Jove's flowers**, which contain the strengths of Jupiter, can facilitate healing, power, and fortune.
- **Chamomile** is said to bring success in gambling.
- **Cinnamon** is sacred to Venus and helps bring good luck.
- **Honeysuckl**e is said to bring psychic powers and creative inspiration, and is one of the most effective of all oils in attracting money.

Basil Bliss

This sweet-tasting herb is excellent in savory dishes. Basil truly grows like a weed and you should cultivate it right on the kitchen windowsill so you can snip and add to your Italian-inspired dishes. Give your basil plants plenty of sun and lots of water, and you will reap a mighty bounty to share with the neighbors. Old wives and hedge witches claim basil protects your home while it brings prosperity and happiness to any gardener's home. Basil helps steady the mind, brings happiness, love, peace, and money, and protects against insanity (what more can you want?). The benefits of this plant are as plentiful as the plant itself; it can be used in getting and attracting love, and on the highest vibrational level, abetting psychic abilities or even astral projection.

Daisy and Echinacea: Healing the Heart and Body

This faithful flower's name is derived from the Anglo-Saxon *daeges eage*, "day's eye" since it closes in the evening. The daisy has been used in one of the oldest love charms. To know if your true love is returned, take a daisy and intone "He loves me, he loves me not" until the last petal is plucked and the answer will be revealed. This flower is not just a boon for romance, however. It is also useful in herbal medicine for aches, bruises, wounds, inflammation, and soothing eye baths. As a flower remedy, it is quite good to help with exhaustion and is a highly regarded remedy in homeopathy. Echinacea is a member of the daisy family that has become wildly popular as a healer for colds and as a powerful immune booster, increasing your T-cell count and fighting off illnesses both minor and major. Echinacea is an herb of abundance, attracting more prosperity, but it can be used in magic workings to amplify the power.

Dandelion Root

The humble dandelion, abhorred by lawn keepers, hides its might well. Dandelion root tea can call upon the spirit of anyone whose advice you might need.

Grind this dried root. Place a tablespoon of the powdered root in a teacup and pour hot water into the cup. Place the brew on your nightstand and say the spirit's name seven times; he or she will visit your dreams and answer your questions. Say the following before going to sleep:

Luck be quick, luck be kind, and, by lucky seven, good luck will be mine. Blessed be.

In Chaucer's day, this method was used to find lost treasures.

Sowing Seeds of Positive Change in Your Life

Nature is the ultimate creator. At a nearby gardening store or hardware store, get an assortment of seed packets to plant newness into your life. If your thumb is not the greenest, try nasturtiums, which are extremely hardy, grow quickly, and spread, beautifying any area. They re-seed themselves, which is a lovely bonus. Light the following candles:

- Green candle and peridot or jade for creativity, prosperity, and growth
- Orange candle and jasper or onyx for clear thinking and highest consciousness
- Blue candle and turquoise or celestine for serenity, kindness, and a happy heart
- White candle and quartz or limestone for purification and safety

Put the seeds under the soil with your fingers and tamp them down gently with your wand, the branch, which you should also stick in the ground at this time. Water your new moon garden and affirmative change will begin in your life that very day.

The Wealth of Wildflowers

Pagans revere poppies for their money magic. If you have a yard, nearby meadow, or any strip of ground you can garden, buy poppy seeds and simply toss half of them all around in early spring. Soon, you will have a wealth of wildflowers. No doubt, you will be rewarded for years to come with the beauty and abundance of poppies for many years to come.

Gather together:

> One small plain paper envelope
> Remaining poppy seeds
> A pen

Place the rest of the poppy seeds in the envelope. Bless the envelope by chanting aloud:

> *Poppy, gold like the sun,*
> *Thank you for the new fortune I've won.*
> *With these words, this spell is sealed. And so it is.*

Now write the charm you have spoken on the envelope. Seal the envelope closed and place it in your wallet, behind your paper money. Your fortunes will begin to change as soon as the envelope is sealed.

Go Forth and Be Fruitful!

Apple

This "one a day" beloved fruit is associated with the goddess Pomona and contains the powers of healing, love, and abundance. Samhain, the high holiday of the Wheel of the Year, is also called the "Feast of Apples" and is used on the Halloween altar during this festival. Cutting an apple in half and sharing the other with your beloved ensures the two of you will stay happy.

Banana

A bunch of bananas packs a magical punch with powers of abundance and fertility for both men and women. Anyone who gets married beneath a banana tree bower will have a lucky marriage. One caveat: never cut a banana, only break it apart. Otherwise, you'll bring back luck to your household.

Blackberry

Blackberries are the medicine that pops up anywhere, offering a delightful snack and serious healing, love, and abundance. Both the vine and the berries can be used for money-bringing spells. Thorny blackberry vines are wonderful as protective wreaths for your home, and the plant vine and berry can be used for prosperity and money spells.

Grapes

Planting grapevines grants you abilities for money magic as well as gardening and farming. The ancient Romans painted pictures of grapes on the garden walls to ensure good harvest and fertility for women. For mental focus, eat some grapes, while magical spell workings for money are abetted greatly by placing a bowl of grapes on the altar.

Pear

It is believed this uniquely shaped fruit brings prosperity and a long life. Somewhat similarly to peaches, the pear creates powers of lust and love. Sharing with a partner, pears can be used to induce sexual arousal. Pear wood is also very good for magical wands.

Pineapple

While renowned as the symbol of hospitality, pineapple represents neighborliness, abundance, and chastity. Dried pineapple in a sachet added to bath water will bring great luck. The juice hinders lust when drunken; dried peel is great in money spells and mixtures.

Tomato

A reminder that the tomato is a fruit! An easy money spell is to place a fresh-off-the-vine tomato on the mantle every few days to bring prosperity. Eating tomatoes inspires love and they're great to grow in your garden as an aid to ward off pests of all kinds!

Love and Money Jam

July is one of the sweetest times to enjoy your garden and strawberries are a harbinger of the good summertimes ahead. To make this lucky jam, get the following ingredients:

    5 cups of strawberries
    1 teaspoon unsalted butter
    1-3/4 ounces) powdered fruit pectin
    7 cups granulated sugar
    1/2 cup fresh basil, chopped
    9 clean and sterilized 1-pint canning jars

Macerate the strawberries in a big bowl. In a large pot, melt the butter and pour in the crushed strawberries. Fold in the powdered pectin. Heat the mixture to a full boil over high heat, stirring constantly. Add in the sugar and bring again to a full rolling boil. Boil and stir for 1 more minute. Now, add in the chopped basil.

Remove the pot from heat and skim off any foam. Ladle the hot mixture into nine half-pint jars, leaving 1/4-inch at the top. Look for and remove any air bubbles. If you need to fill in, add in more hot jam mixture. Carefully wipe the jar rims, then seal the lids on the jars. Place jars into a canner with simmering water, ensuring that they are completely covered with water. Bring to a boil; process for 10 minutes. Remove jars and cool. Strawberries are widely regarded as an aphrodisiac and basil brings money to your house. Making this "Love and Money Jam" will be a great gift to everyone in your household and anyone who is served this jolliest of jams.

Telepathy Tea

The full moon is a perfect time to unleash your prophetic potential when trying to make decisions about investments, job opportunities, or new business ventures. Sharpen your senses with any of these herbal teas:

Borage: A commonplace herb, which is ruled by Jupiter, the planet of abundance.

Mugwort: A favorite of witches for centuries; this is a Venusian infusion.

Yarrow: Drink this before any candle magic for deep knowledge.

Prosperi-tea

Among its healing and energizing properties, the herb berg-amot also brings prosperity. If you are feeling down in the dumps and empty of pocket, fix yourself a pot of bergamot tea and watch the negative energy rise and dissipate with the steam. If a co-worker or boss is exhibiting the same symptoms, fix him some Earl Grey–a fine English tea bursting with precious bergamot.

If the problem runs deeper–no raises, overdue bills, general bitterness–then more systemic healing is necessary. Come to work right before dawn one day. Boil one cup of water and steep a pinch of each of the following dried herbs:

Bergamot: for uplifting energy

Basil: for serenity

Rosemary: for healing

Orange: for joy

When the brew has cooled, rub it on the windowsills, doors, and other places in your workplace where you, your boss, and co-workers can receive the benefits. Things should lighten up right away.

Nature's Talisman

Talismans are charms you can carry with you to help ward off ill fortune and attract the positive toward you. Here is an old-fashioned fetish you can easily make from your pantry and garden.

On the night of the new moon, stuff dried rose, acacia,

and clover into a gold velvet or silk bag. Lastly, place a small magnet in the sack and sew it shut with gold thread. Hold the bag over the smoke of white sage and incense, and meditate to purify your creation. Visualize blessings for you and your loved ones. Carry your lucky talisman with you at all times and begin counting your blessings.

The Power of Poppies

Take a dried poppy seedpod and empty the seeds onto the ground. Take a tiny strip of paper and write down a question about how to attain meaningful and positive rewards in your life. Sleep with the pod and the paper under your pillow. You will experience prophetic dreams that will answer your question. This is best done during the Pisces Moon.

Keep a dream journal by your bed and write down the dream immediately upon waking. Make this a ritual and you will have a rich resource of inner wisdom to guide you.

The Wishing Witching Tree

In Celtic lore, they were called wishing trees, and Taoists referred to them as money trees—either way, they can be giving trees. Plant one in your yard, or pot one for your home or office. If you have to rely on indoor gardening, the biggest focus you can find will do nicely in a jade-green ceramic pot. Choose from among these magical trees, or trust your intuition in arboreal matters:

Willow: for healing broken hearts

Apple: for divination and spellwork

Cherry: for romance

Oak: for strength and lust

Peach: for love magic

Olive: for peace

Aspen: for sensitivity

Eucalyptus: for purification

Herbalist's Astrological Almanac – Plant Healing Wisdom

Plants carry potent energy you can use to amplify your magical workings. Use the signs of the sun, moon, and stars to your advantage, and, over time, you will come to know which ones are most effective for you. Make sure to use your own astrological chart in working with these herbs. Here is a guide to the astrological associations of plants you may grow in your kitchen garden or keep dried in your pantry:

Aries, ruled by Mars: carnation, cedar, clove, cumin, fennel, juniper, peppermint, and pine.

Taurus, ruled by Venus: apple, daisy, lilac, magnolia, oak moss, orchid, plumeria, rose, thyme, tonka bean, vanilla, and violet.

Gemini, ruled by Mercury: almond, bergamot, mint, clover, dill, lavender, lemongrass, lily, and parsley

Cancer, ruled by the Moon: eucalyptus, gardenia, jasmine, lemon, lotus, rose, myrrh, and sandalwood

Leo, ruled by the Sun: acacia, cinnamon, heliotrope, nutmeg, orange, and rosemary

Virgo, ruled by Mercury: almond, cypress, bergamot, mint, mace, moss, thyme, and patchouli

Libra, ruled by Venus: catnip, marjoram, mugwort, spearmint, sweet pea, thyme, and vanilla

Scorpio, ruled by Pluto: allspice, basil, cumin, galangal, and ginger

Sagittarius, ruled by Jupiter: anise, cedar wood, sassafras, star anise, and honeysuckle

Capricorn, ruled by Saturn: lemon thyme, mimosa, vervain, and vetiver

Aquarius, ruled by Uranus: gum, citron, cypress, lavender, spearmint, and pine

Pisces, ruled by Neptune: clover, orris, neroli, sarsaparilla, and sweet pea

Blessing Bag: Herbal Good Luck Charm

Many plants have abundant inherent magic that creates abundance, good fortune, and great good luck. Harvest these herbs and you will hardness the blessings growing in your own back yard.

Gather these supplies:

Small muslin pouch that ties
Teaspoon of basil
Teaspoon of pine needles
Teaspoon of nutmeg
Teaspoon of rosemary
Fennel seed pod
1 vanilla bean pod
3 cinnamon sticks broken into pieces

Take the pouch and stuff it with the herbs. Add the fennel seed and vanilla bean and, lastly, the cinnamon sticks. Tie up the bag, hold it in both hands, and speak the following spell:

I hold in my hands these herbs of providence.
I hold in my heart, these herbs of destiny.
Blessings to all for the good of all.
And so it is. So mote it be.

Tie the bag to the back door of your home or wherever is closest to your plantings. Every time the door opens or closes, the little bag will deliver more good luck.

seven

revenue rocks

Lucky Crystals and Stones of
Security

Gems are powerful tools that can pave the way for a
better life for you. There is a long history of the use
of gems, stones, and crystals as amulets, symbols,
charms, and jewelry in magic. These myriad stones can enrich
your life in so many ways. In the next chapter, you will learn
how to make your own magical gem and crystal jewelry and
how to charge the stones you already own with supernatural
power.

Do you want to get a new job? Jade jewelry magic will do
the trick! Need to get over a heartbreak? A chrysocolla heart-
healing spell will soothe your soul. Are you an author suffering
from the dreaded writer's block? A creativity crystal incantation is exactly what you need.

Gems and statues positioned in strategic places around
your home can help accelerate the positive vibrations you are
activating by practicing crystal and gem magic. Using what I
call crystal feng shui, you can place a crystal, geode, or an
appealingly shaped rock in the appropriate position of your
home to facilitate change. For example, amethyst will promote
healing and release any negative energy that is clinging. Clus-

ters of citrine will activate vibrations of abundance and creativity.

Crystal Magic and How It Works

Crystal magic also involves color magic and spell craft, topics that are covered in depth herein. With crystal magic, you will learn to improve your life in ways large and small. You will discover the stones that are special to you and how to fully utilize these birthstones and karmic crystals. You will undertake the magical arts of crystal conjuring and spell casting with stones. You will be inducted into the practice of healing with crystals and learn how to achieve wellness every day. Finally, you will have at your fingertips the history, description, and instructions on how to use each and every gem and crystal.

Using gems and crystals in rituals, spells, and affirmations has been part of the human experience for millennia. By incorporating this practice into your life, you will create a flow of positive energy that will enable you to enhance your work, your family, your love, and every other part of your existence.

Yes, through the magic of gems, anything is possible. Again, welcome to this glittering and magical realm, and begin a special journey under a sky where every star is a jewel you can wish upon!

Lodestones

Stones, crystals, and gems are regarded as the purest form of the earth's abundance. Whenever you get a new piece of jewelry with a stone or gem, or if you decorate your home or garden with rocks and pebbles, show gratitude for this gift from nature. Sprinkle thyme, marigold blossoms, and ground cinnamon on your garden path and your front doorstep. Also, burn this mix in your incense holder on your alter and chant:

*Mother Nature, I thank you for the strength and bounty
of your bones and stones. Your beauty is reflected now
and forever.
Blessed be.*

Investing in Gold

Pyrite, or fool's gold, is the ideal heart stone for people who
work with money, anyone who is an investor, banker, or
money manager. Stunning and shiny, pyrite has a hardness of
six, the number sacred to Venus. Pyrite brings great luck, along
with abundance and an atmosphere conducive to joy. Delight
everyone at work by keeping a chunk of fool's gold on your
desk. They will think it is a cool decoration, which it certainly
is, and may never guess you have it there to ensure business is
good with stable income.

Kitchen Witch Practical Magic

Any good witch knows that the best ingredients can be found
in your kitchen or your own backyard. Many plants now
thought of as weeds have great healing powers and magical
properties. Most of the herbs and essential oils in this book
have become quite commonplace. With the plethora of
aromatherapy products now available, most oil essences and
scented candles can be bought commercially. For the more
unusual ingredients, try your local health food market, herbal-
ist, or metaphysical store.

Pouch of Plenty: Crystal Charm Bags

A charm bag is a little bag or pouch filled with objects charged
with magic for a specific intent. You can charge them by
placing them on your altar for 24 hours or with spell work.

Gather together:

Small muslin or cloth bags/pouch (that could fit in the palm of your hand)
3 pebble-sized crystals of green jade or peridot or turquoise
1 cinnamon stick
Bolline
Dried basil leaves, one teaspoonful
Green candle
Thyme or cinnamon incense
A length of green cord or string, a foot in length

Set the string aside and place everything else on your altar. Stand at your altar and light a green candle and thyme or cinnamon incense. Pick up the pouch and smudge it in the sweet smoke of the incense while saying the following spell:

My life is blessed and this I know.
Into this bag, prosperity will flow.
I see the future is bright wherever I go,
My life is blessed; this much I know.
With harm to none; so mote it be.

Using your bolline, cut the cinnamon stick into three pieces. Cut the green cord into 3 pieces. Place the basil, pebbles, and cinnamon into the pouch. Now take the green cord, one length at a time, and tie at the end of the bag securely, wrapping it around six times and with a bow. Keep it with you in your pocket and into your life, money will flow.

5 Minute Magic: Turquoise Wish-Spell

Another charm for solvency is to take seven tiny turquoise

stones in the palm of your hand and speak this wish spell aloud:

Luck be quick,
luck be kind,
and, by lucky seven,
good luck will be mine.
Blessed be.

Place the seven small stones in your wallet or purse; more cash is on the way.

Precious Stones Spell

Another charm for solvency is to take seven tiny turquoise stones and put them on your window sill during a full moon for seven hours. Then pick up the stones and, while holding them in the palm of your hand, speak this wish-spell aloud:

The warmth of the sun brings me luck.
The light of the stars sends me fortune.
In this crystal, the energy of abundance is stored.
I wish for plenty for all. I wish for plenty for me.
And do it is!

Tranquility Touchstones: Crystal Cairns

I am sure you will come to find this to be true: certain crystals can be touchstones in your life and bring multitudinous benefits, both emotional and spiritual. Find spots in your home or office where you can incorporate them into your every day, whether at a shrine, on your nightstand, or stacked in a corner on your desk as a sort of crystal cairn. This can be your special corner of the world where you can renew and connect with your spiritual center. Picking up and holding your touch-stones can be one of the most soul-nourishing small acts of self-care you can do.

Following is a list of different crystals and what their presence will bring you:

Inspiration: Amazonite, aventurine, carnelian, chrysolite, chrysoprase, citrine, green tourmaline, malachite, yellow fluorite

Intuition: amethyst, azurite, celestite, lapis lazuli, moonstone, selenite, smoky quartz, sodalite, star sapphire, yellow calcite

Love: amethyst, magnetite, rhodochrosite, rose quartz, twinned rock crystals

Abundance: bloodstone, carnelian, citrine, dendritic agate, diamond, garnet, hawk's-eye, moss agate, peridot, ruby, tigers-eye, topaz, yellow sapphire

Protection: amber, apache tear, chalcedony, citrine, green calcite, jade, jet, smoky quartz

Self-belief: azurite, chalcedony, chrysocolla, green tourmaline, hematite, rutilated quartz, tiger's-eye

Serenity: amber, aventurine, blue jade, dioptase, Herkimer diamond, jasper, kunzite, moonstone, onyx, peridot, quartz, rhodonite

Confidence: carnelian, obsidian, quartz, selenite, sodalite, topaz

Positive Energy: agate, aventurine, bloodstone, calcite, chalcedony, citrine, dioptase, emerald, garnet, orange calcite, ruby, topaz

Deep wisdom: emerald, fluorite, Herkimer diamond, moldavite, serpentine, yellow calcite

Dream Crystals

Thomas Edison carried quartz crystals with him at all times and called the stones his dream crystals. He believed they inspired his ideas and inventions. Literary legends George Sand and William Butler Yeats also relied on crystals to help spark their considerable creativity.

Data has also been gathered to show the effectiveness of quartz in certain healing techniques, such as chakra therapy, acupressure, and light-ray therapy, as we will discuss in depth later. But the simplest way to promote healing with crystal is to wear a stone.

Quartz can take the form of great hexagonal stones or crystals so small that only a microscope can see them. Quartz can appear in clusters or singly. It can also appear in every hue of the rainbow. The gorgeous and varied hues of quartz come from electrostatic energy, which now can be altered through technology. I, however, prefer the simple beauty provided by Mother Nature herself.

Quartz is the largest of the crystal families, and we can be grateful for that since it is such a powerful healer. Moreover, it is an energy regulator for the human body, affecting the vibrations of the *aura*, or energy field that surrounds all living beings.

Gifted and Talented: Success Accessories for Work

It is no accident that kings, queens, and emperors wore crowns. The ancients expected their leaders to be wise, and a bejeweled crown bestowed the brilliance and power of the gems to the crowned person. While you may not want to wear a tiara to the office or a crown to the grocery store, you can wear hair clips and barrettes with crystals and stones attached for some of the same reasons. Why not be smarter and smartly accessorized? Bejeweled barrettes worn at the temples confer wit and wisdom, a kind of brain-boosting power energy.

Astrogemology: Signs and Stones

Each astrological sign is associated with at least one precious gem, or soul stone, one power stone, and one heart stone. The most precious gem for each sign is another kind of birthstone, the jewel marking entry into the world—a guide for your life, if you will. Power stones are lucky omens and heart stones are the more affordable of crystals, so we can all afford to keep them in our homes, on our desks, and in our bedrooms. I highly recommend them as altar crystals.

Aries, *First Half: March 20–April 3*

Pink diamond is the soul stone of choice for early-born Aries. Among the rarest of all diamonds, pink diamonds became a huge fad in late 2002, when actor Ben Affleck gave one to lady love Jennifer Lopez as her engagement ring. They are both Leos, but no matter! Aries babies are ruled by the planet Mars. The finest-quality pink diamonds usually come from Western

Australia. A secondary precious-crystal stone for this part of Aries is the pink sapphire, also rare.

Sunstone is the power crystal for these Aries folks. Appropriately red with an iridescent glow, sunstone is a gold-flecked good-luck charm for the Mars-ruled. Jasper and heliotrope are the other power stones for this part of the year. These red rocks will amp up your lust for life.

The heart stones for these zodiac pioneers are dolomite, rose quartz, and cinnabar. So, Aries, put rose quartz by your bedside for self-esteem, self-love, and spiritual comfort.

Aries, *Last Half: April 4-April 18*

Alexandrite is the designated soul stone here. It is not as rare as pink diamond but is very precious indeed—the scarcest of the chrysoberyls. Usually a dark green, alexandrite shows red under certain types of light. This royal stone is fitting for the first sign of the zodiac. Another soul stone for later-born Aries is rhodonite, a pinkish-red crystal that's a favorite of Carl Faberge's. This is a bringer of great wealth.

The power stone for this half of Aries is bowenite, a stone of great strength in a mossy green. While many of the crystals assigned to late Aries are red or pink, this one is green, signifying the other side of the planet Mars. Bowenite is especially precious and sacred to the Maori of New Zealand, where some of the finest specimens come from, and was highly prized by the ancient Indians and Persians. Carnelian is second in line as a power stone and was commonly carved ceremoniously by the Egyptians, the Greeks, and the Phoenicians in the pre-Christian era. Egyptians loved scarabs carved out of the umber-colored chalcedony. Explore the cavalcade of crystal stores on the Internet to find yourself a carnelian carved scarab for a personal power boost.

The heart stone for later-born Aries is the pale pink iridescent stone known as the youngite, which looks like a lighter-colored red jasper. One thousand years before Christ, the Egyptians made much jewelry out of this heart stone.

Taurus, *First Half: April 19-May 2*

Emerald is the soul stone for those born in the first half of this luxury-loving and Venus-ruled sign. Tauruses are frequently very good with managing wealth and investments, so it makes sense that emeralds are the color of money. If you are an early-born Taurus, you would do well to obtain an emerald and wear it to work and to the bank for enhancing energy.

The power stone for this group is another gorgeous green stone, malachite, which also corresponds to the planet Venus. An earthy rock, it is befitting for this earth sign of the zodiac and has many magical tales to its credit. A malachite heart pendant or paperweight is perfect for early Tauruses.

Pyrite, or fool's gold, is the heart stone for people in this family, who, again, tend to be bankers and money managers. Stunning and shiny, pyrite has a hardness of six, the number sacred to Venus. Pyrite brings great luck to early Tauruses along with abundance and an atmosphere conducive to joy. Delight everyone at work by keeping a chunk of fool's gold on your desk.

Taurus, *Second Half: May 3-May 19*

Andalusite is the precious soul stone here, a magically metamorphic crystal. Tauruses are deeply rooted to the earth, and andalusite represents that elemental energy through its range of colors, from earthy black to clear and watery. In fact, andalusite comes in nearly all the colors of the rainbow (yellow, green, red, purple, brown, and gray), manifesting another Venusian quality—glamour.

Jadeite, the power money stone for later Tauruses, also comes in many colors. Jadeite is a symbol of abundance and permanence. Jadeite rings with a lovely tone when struck, representing the natural musical talent possessed by members of this sign. A jadeite bracelet, ring, or bowl is essential for the May-born.

Tauruses in this group have a most whimsical heart stone, the Irish fairy stone. This is a mutable crystal made up of several elements: bluish galena, clear quartz crystal, yellow sphalerite, and pyrite. While Irish fairy stone is composed of these different stones, it has its own unique qualities of endurance and stability. This stone brings many blessings to the May Tauruses.

Gemini, *First Half: May 20-June 4*

Orange sapphire has long been associated with communication, specifically the telling of truths. As a soul stone, it can help early-half Geminis achieve the mastery of communication that is their karmic due. Sapphires are the hardest of gems after diamonds. In India of old, the orange sapphire was prized beyond any other; it was called padparad-scha, the Sanskrit word for lotus blossom. The Chaldeans associated this stone with this sign after observing the orange tint of the planet Mercury, the ruler of Gemini.

Moss agate, quartz with a plantlike pattern caused by metallic crystalline grains, is the power money stone for first-half Geminis and represents the dualism of this sign of the Twins. The ancients actually thought the dark green markings inside the stone were fossilized moss. They used moss agate for water divining, so it was especially sacred to farmers. It is associated with the metal-rich planet Mercury and makes a great grounding stone for members of this air sign, who need to keep their feet on the ground.

The heart stone for early Geminis is staurolite, named from the Greek word *staurus*, which translates to "cross." Staurolite forms a natural crucifix because of the way the iron molecules in the stone line up. Bright red is one of the colors associated with Geminis, and staurolite most commonly appears in this vibrant color, causing it to be mistaken for garnet. This stone can help Geminis align with their true purpose, so they will benefit from keeping it at their bedsides or on their desks.

Gemini, *Second Half: June 5-June 20*

Cat's-eye, the lovely golden yellow gem, is the special soul stone for late-born Geminis. The ancient Greeks, who called this crystal cymophane, meaning "waving light," believed this stone guarded against danger to the soul and the body. The iridescent surface of the stone causes it to appear in different colors; the shade depends on the angle from which the cat's-eye is being seen. This mutable stone reflects back to Geminis their changeable nature and helps them to acknowledge their quicksilver personalities and to grow from that deep recognition. Geminis, wear a cat's-eye ring and see your soul reflected back at you.

Late Geminis can count on the garnet known as Transvaal jade, or grossular, for their power. People most often think of garnets as red stones of great clarity, but this specimen is opaque and a beautiful bright green. Under certain light, it appears as a blazing yellow color. This ability to change color symbolizes the dual nature of the June-born. Originating many millions of years ago in the deep core of the earth, Transvaal jade contains many metals in its makeup, a fact that also corresponds to the Gemini nature of having so many different qualities and talents. Wearing this garnet can awaken hidden talents in Geminis and bring them to the fore.

Geode, which usually comes in two split halves, is the ideal power money stone for later-born Geminis, but they must have both halves to help integrate the two parts of their nature and make for a complete, whole person. Geodes are formed from old volcanic bubbles and are usually solid agate outside with a center of gorgeous amethyst, opal, or rock crystal. If you are a Gemini, I recommend keeping one of the geode halves at home on your altar or in a special spot where you can see it every day and the other half at your place of work, to reflect and connect the two parts of your nature.

Tips 'n' Tricks: Twin Hearts

Many crystal shops and New Age stores now feature heart-shaped rocks. The next time you see heart-shaped amethyst crystals, buy two right away and give one to your true love. The gift of an amethyst heart will ensure a happy life together and good fortune shared. Sweet!

Cancer, *First Half: June 21-July 4*

Cancers are ruled by the Moon, so it is appropriate that moonstone is the precious soul stone for the individuals born in the first half of this sign. The most priceless of moonstones is adularia, named after the place it was first discovered— Adula, Switzerland. Moonstones have an opalescent sheen reminiscent of the Moon in the night sky. Adularia was special to early Europeans who believed it could improve the memory, help stop seizures, overcome a broken heart, and foretell the future. Wearing moonstone jewelry will put Cancers in tune with their lunar-influenced changeable natures, giving them strength and the wisdom of intuition.

Pearl is the power money stone of great price for early Cancers. Pearls have a long and rich history; they were first written about in China 4,000 years ago and were celebrated in all the ancient cultures of the world after humankind first opened a shell and found the prize inside. Cancers are the great historians of the zodiac, and they have incredible memories. They are connected to pearls because of a common link with the ocean and the tides, which are regulated by Cancer's ruler, the Moon. If you are a Cancer, honor your native element, water, by wearing pearls on occasion (but not constantly), and by decorating your home and workspace with shells. This will help you stay secure, refreshed, and relaxed and help you avoid your great nemesis: worry.

Calcite, made up of many fossilized seashells, is the heart stone for first-half Cancers. Because the ocean makes up so much of the surface of the planet (and encompassed even more area in the first few million of Earth's years), calcite is common, but there are many lovely specimens, such as Iceland spar, flos ferri, and nailhead calcite. Iceland spar is a beautiful clear type of calcite, and when you look at it from certain angles you can see a double image. Nailhead calcite shows many small, rounded circles of variegated colors. Flos ferri, maybe the most beautiful of the three calcite stones, boasts fragile, white, treelike branches that take on other colors when exposed to different minerals. Cancers, scatter this Moon-ruled rock all around your homes for grounding and healing.

Cancer, *Second Half: July 5-July 21*

Opal is the power money stone for later-born Cancers. Opals can't be duplicated artificially due to the complicated nature of their patterning, varying hues, and play of color. The most precious of all opals feature a star, called an asterism. Opals are mysterious, just like Cancers, having much depth beneath their protective shells. The ancients exulted about opals; Pliny the Elder wrote, "For in them you shall see the living fire of ruby, the glorious purple of the amethyst, the sea-green of the emerald, all glittering together in an incredible mixture of light." Cancer, you will come into your soul's true purpose by wearing opal jewelry.

Red coral is the power stone for the second half of Cancer. It is formed by lime secreted by sea creatures to create their homes. One memorable old story associated with the oceanic gem is the ancient Greek belief that sea sprites stole Medusa's severed head and took it to the bottom of the sea, and that each drop of her blood formed a red coral. The stone was believed to be healing and protective then, and it still is today. For Cancers, red coral is good for vitality and is a symbol of life and love and health. Wear red coral beads over your heart and you will immediately feel vibrant.

Desert rose, formed of cemented sand particles, is the heart stone for this group of Cancers. The Saharan Bedouin believed it was formed from the tears of women mourning for those who had died in battle. Desert rose is gypsum originating in lake bottoms that have become desert and comes in beautiful earth tones of red, yellow, gray, brown, and pink. For later Cancers, this heart stone helps contain and release emotions in a healthy, expressive way. Decorate your bedroom, your inner sanctum, with desert rose for a soothing and calming effect.

Leo, *First Half: July 22-August 5*

Yellow diamond is a brilliant power money stone, befitting the king of the zodiacal wheel. Diamond is pure carbon and the hardest substance on Earth, and its name appropriately originates from the Greek word *adamas*, meaning "invincible." Yellow diamonds represent the Sun, the ruling planet for Leos, and the symbol of this sign's high level of consciousness—true heart, great generosity, and incredible courage. Yellow diamond earrings will keep you Leos in balance.

First-half Leos can count zircon as their power stone. Beloved by early cultures, the brilliant zircon was believed to safeguard against poison and was thought to be a holy healer in India. In the early Roman Catholic church, it was held to be a sign of humility. For Leos, whose downfall can be pride, zircon can guard against this and keep the astrological Lions on an even keel.

Early-born Leos have a special heart stone in lesser-known vandanite, which can be a beautiful red-orange or a glorious yellow-gold. Vandanite is rich in lead and also vanadium, the mineral used to strengthen steel. Vandanite is formed at intense temperatures, which can be related to our Sun, a furnace in the heavens. For Leos, this unusual heart stone can help them deal with the pressure of a lot of attention, which Leos naturally attract with their vibrant and magnetic personalities. You should keep your heart stone at home and at work for optimum stability and inspiration.

Leo, *Second Half: August 6-August 21*

White diamond is the soul gem for late Leos. It is regarded as the purest of all the hard, pure-carbon crystals. Old cultures deemed this diamond a guard against harm and a bringer of great fortune and enlightenment. Gemologists sometimes refer to this stone as "of the first water," in reference to its unmatched purity. The lion is the king of the beasts, and Leo the Lion is zodiacal royalty; white diamond is as hot as the Sun itself. Leos can use this rock in all jewelry to aspire to the greatness within it.

Heliodor, named for Helios, the Greek god of the sun, is the ultimate power stone for second-half Leos. Heliodor, a member of the beryl family, is the sunny yellow sister of the popular green emerald and blue aquamarine. It is formed under extremely high temperatures and pressures. Heliodor can help you Leos call upon your greatest qualities and talents and provide the impetus to go out and try to make your dreams come true!

The heart stone for later-born Leos is the most unexpected— sulfur, called brimstone in biblical times. Sulfur is a very dynamic rock; the crystals enlarge even by the heat of a hand that holds it. If you rub sulfur, it will give off a negative charge. A cluster of sulfur is a luminous mass of gold crystals and is quite beautiful despite the images its name may conjure. Obviously, sulfur is associated with fire and has been used for centuries in explosive materials such as gunpowder, fireworks, and matches. Leo is a fire sign, and Leos can hold emotions in until they ignite and explode. Keeping sulfur at home can help Leos stay balanced and release their energy in healthy and positive ways.

Virgo, *First Half: August 22-September 5*

Black opal is the soul stone for early Virgos. Virgos are perhaps the most discriminating of signs and would relish the fact that until recently, black opals came from only a few acres in Australia. The ancient Romans, seeing the rainbow colors of opals, believed them to be the bridge between heaven and Earth, but they especially desired the few poor-quality black opals (now believed to have been faked) held by the barbarians in Hungary. The finest grade of black opal was discovered on the island of Java, in Indonesia. For Virgos, only the best and only the real black opals will do. Members of the sign of service and help to others, Virgos gain strength and intensity and augment their own purity with black opals. This stone has been called the gem of hope, and, as such, offers a high level of consciousness for Virgos.

The power talisman for first-half Virgos is labradorite, the lovely iridescent stone that originated in Labrador. Like Geminis, Virgos are ruled by Mercury, and the quicksilver, peacock-hued labradorite is good for providing the mental swiftness Virgos need to accomplish all of their goals in life. This type of feldspar can reflect every color of the spectrum and help Virgos from becoming too task-oriented—too focused on one thing. No one can work harder than Virgos, and labradorite can prevent exhaustion from overwork and can also ensure that early Virgos activate a variety of talents.

Magnetite, also known as lodestone, is the optimal heart stone for first-half Virgos. Another glittery, surface-changing rock, magnetite contains a lot of iron, and thanks to its common occurrence and adaptability, it is popular in jewelry. Virgos are associated with health, medicine, and nursing, and magnetite has become a good healing stone because of its magnetic qualities. If you are a Virgo, wear this stone and give it to people you love for good health and prosperity.

Virgo, *Second Half: September 6-September 21*

Virgos in this group celebrate iolite as their precious soul gem, which is associated with their ruling planet Mercury due to its crystalline composition of two dark and two light metallic elements. Iolite is named after the Greek word *ios*, meaning "violet." Formed under enormous pressure in extremely high temperatures, iolite has a high vibration. The stone can help Virgos stay out of career ruts and achieve their true spiritual natures.

Tiger's-eye, another iridescent gem, is the power stone for later Virgos, denoting strength, courage, and perception. Virgos are great critics, missing no flaw, and tiger's-eye can help them to have incredible vision and be able to see the wonderful possibilities in all things.

The heart stone for second-half Virgos is obsidian, a glinting black, extremely hard and tough natural glass formed by volcanic activity. Virgos are always helping other people and sometimes become vulnerable because of this. Using obsidian as home decoration can help them keep all of their energy from going to others and causing imbalance. Some obsidians have stripes; in ancient Mexico, where obsidian was plentiful, the striped variety was believed to prevent negative, or dark, magic. Virgos can be extremely self-critical, and having obsidian nearby can absorb their negativity and help turn it positive. This is an essential stone for the September-born!

Libra, *First Half: September 22-October 6*

A soul stone that was extremely popular in days of old is spinel, a jewel available in a multitude of hues, including black, dark green, orange, white, blue, purple, and red. Spinels were symbols and stones of the royals; the Queen of England owned a grand specimen called the Timur ruby, and the czars of Russia wore a crown decorated with a magnificent spinel. Spinels are rarer than either rubies or sapphires, and I predict they will have a renaissance. The extremely rare precious green spinel is the type most highly prized among Libras, and it can bring out their aesthetic values and empower their pursuit of the arts.

Dioptase is the power stone for first-half Libras. A deeper green than any emerald, it has an extensive copper content. Venus is associated with the color green, and the intensity of this gorgeous green stone makes it a love crystal for Venus-ruled Libras, enriching both their personal relationships and their higher love for humankind. Dioptase can also awaken the spiritual side of Libras, making the usually attractive members of this sign even more beautiful inside and out. Dioptase is difficult to cut for jewelry because of its brittleness. Use uncut crystal clusters as lovely spirit enhancers all around the home.

Kyanite is the sky-colored heart stone for early Libras. Because it shares the same chemistry (but different crystal structure) as a couple of other minerals, kyanite is known as a stone of symmetry, perfect for providing balance. The Greeks favored this aluminum-based rock and called it disthene, meaning "dual strength," because it is soft (and easily cut) lengthwise but much harder across. Kyanite most commonly occurs in long, bluish-green crystal blades but also comes in cluttered rosettes with a pearly, opalescent surface. If you're a Libra, an air sign, keep kyanite around to stay steady and strong and help avoid spreading yourself too thin and succumbing to petty, energy-draining distractions.

Libra, *Second Half: October 7-October 22*

Blue sapphire, exceedingly rare and of exceptionally high quality, is the soul gem of choice for later-born Libras. The name "sapphire" has several origins, among them *sapphirus,* the Latin word for blue. The blue in the stone comes from the iron and titanium inside. This gem represents Venus's glinting blue in the blue-black of the darkened heavens. Libras are great romantics, and blue sapphire's high vibration of love can activate their creativity so they can craft great works of art—songs, poetry, paintings, and anything their imaginations can conceive.

The power talisman for this group of Libras is jadeite, sometimes called imperial green jade. The Chinese highly prize this stone in their lengthy history and culture and believe it contains all that you need for a happy, long life—courage, modesty, charity, wisdom, and, most importantly for the Libra scales to be in balance, justice. Jade bookends on your desk are perfect balancers.

. . .

Limonite, an icicle-like mineral appearing in long, shiny pieces, is the heart stone for second-half Libras. This represents the striving for a higher mind, higher beauty, and higher love necessary for the completion of Libra karma.

Scorpio, *First Half: October 23-November 6*

The soul stone for early Scorpios is ruby, a gem celebrated in many legends dating from prehistoric times to the present day. Rubies were believed to be dragons' eggs—very fitting for Scorpios, who have a lizard aspect to their souls. Rubies were believed to give the wearers invincibility. They were also thought to warn of danger by darkening in shade to a red that was nearly black. Rubies correspond to Mars, the first ruling planet of Scorpio, also associated with red. The most valuable rubies outrank even diamonds, and in the Bible, ruby is called the most precious of the gems first created in the world. If worn by a Scorpio, a ruby can rechannel passions such as lust, jealousy, and anger into more positive emotions. By all means, wear rubies, soulful Scorpios!

First-half Scorpios have a most unusual power stone in blue John. It is found in only one place in the world: the underground caverns beneath a hill in the county of Derbyshire, England. The Roman emperor Nero was crazy for it and paid an enormous price for a single vase made from it. It is the rarest of the fluorites, and its appearance of dark blue and reddish purple bands on a white background relates to Pluto, the second ruling planet of Scorpio. This is the sign of the underworld and secrets, and the origin of the name of its talisman is a mystery no one has yet solved. Though blue John can be difficult to come by, other fluorites are more readily available and will substitute nicely for the rare stone. Fluorite is thought to be healing to the bones and to wounds that lie underneath the surface. Secretive Scorpios carry many hurts beneath strong exteriors, and fluorites can gently resolve these over time.

For early Scorpios, the heart stone is stibnite, a blue-gray mineral that comes in clusters of needle-like rods. Stibnite is closely associated with Pluto and has a shiny and opalescent surface. It is soft, and because of its crumbliness, stibnite greatly alleviates this, making it easier for Scorpios to get along with other people and get along better in the world. If you're a Scorpio, you know you have a strong will; this stone can help you get your ideas across without forcing them. A chunk of stibnite on your desk at work will help your career and reputation.

Scorpio, *Second Half: November 7-November 21*

Rhodochrosite is the precious soul stone for later Scorpios. Once called rosinca, or Inca rose, this pink beauty takes its color from iron, magnesium, and calcium. Rhodochrosite corresponds to the planets Mars, Pluto, and the Moon. The gem is formed over a very long period of time under relatively gentle geological circumstances and therefore has a gentle energy that calms the volcanic passions and anger that commonly erupts in Scorpios. As mentioned previously, Scorpios carry so much under the surface in silence. This gem can enable you to express your feelings healthily.

. . .

Everybody thinks of amethyst as the February crystal for Aquarians and Pisceans, but it is also the power stone for second-half Scorpios. The purple color related to the purple planet, Pluto. Amethyst can open the love vibration for individuals ruled by this most misunderstood and enormously powerful water sign. Wearing amethyst jewelry and keeping chunks of amethyst crystal in the home and workplace can reveal the sweet, funny, smart, approachable, and lovable side of Scorpios, offering them a much greater chance for happiness.

Scorpios have their heart stone in the very available quartz crystal. Quartz is a tremendous healer, and so are Scorpios, though they rarely receive credit for this latent talent. When a Scorpio puts her mind to something, nothing can stand in the way! By acknowledging and utilizing the healing power of quartz crystal, Scorpios can use their personal power for the good of others and greatly benefit. Surround yourself with this inexpensive heat crystal and feel the love.

Sagittarius, *First Half: November 22-December 5*

Tourmaline—specifically the multihued specimen known as melonstone, which is pinkish red with a blue-green stripe—is the precious soul stone for the Jupiter-ruled Sagittarians. Individuals under this fire sign are lively and very action-oriented, and tourmaline, which readily gives off an electrical charge when warmed, can match and propel their energy. Tourmaline is the stone for adventurers and explorers. Get some today and hit the road, dear Sag.

. . .

Amber is the power stone for early Sagittarians. This rock formed from fossilized tree sap and resin, an organic crystal. Amber was thought by the ancients to have trapped the sun, and it was called electron by the Greeks, who observed its negative electrical charge. Even wildly active Sagittarians should wear this stone only on special occasions. It keeps energy cycling within, which is good, but it can have a weakening effect if worn all the time. Amber helps performers; actors and musicians swear by it.

Chrysocolla is the heart stone for first-half Sagittarians. Either blue or green, this copper-rich crystal is one of great life-giving vibrancy. Sagittarians always have many irons in many fires and often burn up their energy in typical fire-sign style. Chrysocolla can help prevent this and help Sagittarians direct their energy toward more purposeful and heartfelt pursuits.

Sagittarius, *Second Half: December 5-December 20*

Tourmaline is also the soul stone for later-born Sagittarians. (See "Sagittarius, First Half," above.)

Turquoise is this group's power stone. The rock has a rich and colorful history and was valued in the extreme by Persians, Egyptians, Mexicans, Bedouins, Chinese, Tibetans, Native Americans, and Turks. Turquoise is associated with horses and riders; Sagittarius is the centaur of the zodiac—half man and half horse. Once revered as the eye of Ra, the Egyptian sun god, turquoise lends sight and aids in travel. Wearing this stone will help people born in this part of the year to find their purpose and harness the passion and vision to see it through.

. . .

The heart stone for second-half Sagittarians is bornite, a burnished red rock of copper and iron. Bornite used to be called peacock ore because of its impressive iridescent coloration. It is a very powerful energy crystal. Although it is not widely known, Sagittarians can be indecisive, and this stone abets them in overcoming that. This is also a stone of justice; Jupiter-ruled Sagittarians are lovers of justice.

Capricorn, *First Half: December 21-January 6*

Topaz in any of its color incarnations is the soul stone for early Capricorns. Topaz gained its name from sailors who found it while exploring the desert island upon which they were ship-wrecked. They named both the stone and the island Topazos, translating to mean "lost and then found." With Topaz, ambi-tious Capricorns will leave no stone unturned in the path to glory.

For power stones, first-half Goats have both lazulite and jet, gems that have a dark and shadowy appearance representative of Saturn, Capricorn's ruling planet. Jet is one of the oldest stones known to man, fitting with the longevity of the slow and steady Capricorns, reputed to grow more youthful as they get older. Wear jet to live long and prosper!

Citrine and smoky quartz are the heart stones for this sector of the zodiac and will ground this hardworking earth sign. Keep citrine at your place of work and wear citrine rings and neck-laces frequently to remain in touch with your feelings.

. . .

Capricorn, *Second Half: January 7-January 19*

Tanzanite is the sacred soul stone for these Capricorns. A gorgeous purple stone found in 1967 Tanzania, it corresponds to the ruling planet of Saturn. Appropriately regal and rare, it is as serious as the sign it signifies. For important meetings and moments in your life, a tanzanite jewel will make you a shining star!

Lucky Goats in the latter half of Capricorn get to have lapis lazuli as their talismanic power crystal. This crystal was absolutely revered by the Egyptians and other Mesopotamian cultures. A bright blue, this stone connotes wisdom, accomplishment, and value. I highly suggest lots of lapis boxes, jewelry, and figurines for full steam ahead.

Rock crystal is a most practical heart stone for these Capricorns. Known as the salt of the earth, this form of quartz is fairly common but is also perhaps the single most effective and most often used stone in magic. I have been seeing many rock crystal lamps lately that give a beautiful flow and pleasurable negative ions. Decorate with these lamps and you'll go far and feel good with the process.

Aquarius, *First Half: January 20-February 3*

Olivine is the soul gem of choice for first-half Aquarians, and it is a stone with a royal heritage. The Egyptians believed this peridot to be the stone of the gods. The long, convoluted, and quite bizarre history of this stone entirely suits Aquarians, who are ruled by Uranus, the planet of chaos and unexpected change. Wear a dark green olivine on momentous occasions to mark them as special in your life.

Onyx, the deep, dark power stone for early Aquarians, was beloved by peoples of prehistory and by craftsmen of the classical era. Onyx is super for grounding you airy Aquarians!

The heart stone for this group is moldavite. With its otherworldly origin as a meteorite, it is perfect for the Uranian bolt-from-the-blue these scientist-philosophers represent. Moldavite is a mysterious and powerful crystal with many mist-shrouded legends and theories. No doubt, an Aquarius will get to the bottom of them all one day. Moldavite will add to your Aquarian brilliance and boost your personal creativity to new heights.

Aquarius, *Second Half: February 4-February 18*

Diopside is the beautiful blue soul stone for later-born Aquarians. This stone has ties to both Uranus, the official ruling planet of Aquarius, and Saturn, the sign's ruler before Uranus was discovered. In 1964, star diopside, an included type, was found; it is a magical and stunningly gorgeous stone that has a quality of electric enlightenment, just like these February-born inventors, artists, and visionary businesspeople.

Late Aquarians have jade as a power stone. It is a universal healer and love stone that can keep these very intellectually oriented people in touch with their hearts and bodies.

The heart stone for second-half Aquarians is charoite, a purple mineral that corresponds with Venus, Saturn, and Uranus. This is a fairly recent rock, perfect for the modern-minded February-born, who are generally fifty years ahead of everyone else. Chaorite was discovered circa 1947 near the Chara River in Russia and was immediately greeted as a very special stone for the new centuries.

Pisces, *First Half: February 19-March 4*

I have a vested interest in the gem lore regarding Pisces as my birthday is February 19! The sign of the Fishes is affected by the moons of three planets: Triton, Neptune's largest moon; Io, one of Jupiter's moons; and our moon here on Earth. Because Pisces is represented by a pair of fish, members of the first half of this sign share two different soul stones. The first is the oceanic blue-green diamond, associated with Neptune, the ruling planet of Pisces. Aquamarine, which relates to all three of the afore-mentioned moons, is the second soul stone for Fishes. Aquamarine was once believed to be the dried tears of sea nymphs. It is the purest, most harmonious energy-enhancing stone for Pisceans; wear it and you will stay in the swim.

For their power talisman, early Pisceans have a mutable rock, smithsonite, a soft, calcium-based stone that comes in a variety of lovely pastel colors. It is a stone for creativity, the bailiwick of this sign. Keep smithsonite at your easel, drawing table, or writing desk.

Opal fossils, the heart stones for these sensitive people, are ancient fragments that crystallized and achieved iridescence through an accumulation of water and minerals over time. Pisces is, of course, a water sign and is also associated with history and deep, old wisdom.

Pisces, *Second Half: March 4–March 19*

The soul gem for the very end of the zodiac is kunzite, a very lovely lilac-rose-colored stone that was discovered at the very beginning of the twentieth century, about one minute ago in geological terms. Before the planet Neptune was discovered, Pisces shared its former ruling planet, Jupiter, with Sagittarius; kunzite is *Jovian* (relating to Jupiter) gem. It is a sensitive stone, which befits sensitive people. Kunzite will help you face this pressure-filled world and stay above the fray with grace.

The power stone for late Pisces is the chrysoprase, a gem that has been revered throughout the ages. Chrysoprase was assigned sovereignty and utilized by high priests of nearly every era. This crystal is perfect for the sign that can attain the highest level of spiritual evolution. With chrysoprase, you can help others and yourself through soul attunement.

Late Pisceans can count as their heart stone the all-purpose fluorite, which comes in a rainbow of colors corresponding to the rainbow gills of fish. This stone is found all over our planet and is so universally helpful that it presents a solid foundation for gentle Pisceans. Fluorite at home and work will add comfort and grace to your space.

Tips 'n' Tricks: Stones for Success

If you need to up your ambition, these are the stones to paving the path to prosperity for everyone:

- **Azurite** strengthens mental powers.
- **Chalcedony** gives you get-up-and-go!
- **Emerald** aids in problem solving.
- **Opal** encourages faithful service.
- **Pearl** engenders material wealth.
- **Quartz** helps overcome fear of rejection.
- **Sapphire** helps with goal setting.
- **Tourmaline** promotes an attitude of accomplishment

conclusion: spellcasting a happy, healthy, and wealthy life

Dear Friend,

When I moved to California from Appalachia right after grad school, I was not prepared for how different the cost of living was. Rents were more than double, and food and even gas for your car were much more expensive. I was in shock but also had to work swiftly to be able to keep a roof over my head, gas in the car for the commute across the Bay Bridge to work, and food quickly became an issue. I was renting a room that has been a closet in a gloriously dingy Victorian on Haight Street. It was fun yet fiscally stressful. My mother brought me up to be very self-sufficient and also to never borrow money. When even a 2 dollar slice of pizza from the joint down the street became too much for my minuscule budget, I used my last coins to buy a bag of apples and a bag of potatoes and lived on that and herbal tea for two long weeks until I got paid from my job again. And from that not-so-big check, was not only grocery and gas money, but also the last sum needed for a first and last month's security deposit to get my own humble apartment in the Lower Haight district of San Francisco.

I had scrimped and saved and literally pinched pennies to buy that bag of apples and potatoes. But, it was all worth it as I knew in my bones that I would have a cozy little home I could make my own and share with loved ones and all the new friends I was making. Finally, I had my own space where I would endeavor on magical workings, hold spiritual gatherings, concoct myriad brews, candles, and other tools of the craft, and I also started collecting used paperbacks to build my library of esoterica, which I treasure to this day. I immediately set about creating abundance in my life and many of the spells in this book are ones I used to create a comfortable home, professional success, and enough money to save, invest, and eventually buy a home as well as tithe to good causes.

I sincerely want the same for you and intend for you to have a life filled with blessings and happiness.

And here is what I know: you have all you need within you to do just that. You are a magical being and deserve a life filled with joy, prosperity, and great good health that is overflowing with love!

Blessed be! xo

Cerridwen Greenleaf

resources

Ritual Resources:

Planetary, Lunar, Astrological, Numeric, Herbal and Deity Correspondences

Deepen your magical workings and spellcasting success by applying this wisdom.

Dates and Times

-

This section contains lists and tables of information you can use to cast spells and work magic using dates, planets, goals, and astrological signs (if a date is listed as being both lucky and unlucky, the ritualist is free to make his or her own decision regarding personal practice).

Four Major Sabbats:

Candlemas—February 2

Beltane—May 1

Lammas—August 1

Samhain—October 31

Four Lesser Sabbats:
Vernal Equinox—March 20
Summer Solstice—June 24
Autumn Equinox—September 23
Winter Solstice/Yule—December 21

Lucky and Unlucky Dates

Month: January
Lucky Dates: 3, 10, 27, 31
Unlucky Dates: 12, 23

Month: February
Lucky Dates: 7, 8, 18
Unlucky Dates: 2, 10, 17, 22

Month: March
Lucky Dates: 3, 9, 12, 14, 16
Unlucky Dates: 13, 19, 23, 28

Month: April
Lucky Dates: 5, 17
Unlucky Dates: 18, 20, 29, 30

Month: May
Lucky Dates: 1, 2, 4, 6, 9, 14
Unlucky Dates: 10, 17, 20

Month: June
Lucky Dates: 3, 5, 7, 9, 13, 23
Unlucky Dates: 4, 20

Month: July
Lucky Dates: 2, 6, 10, 23, 30
Unlucky Dates: 5, 13, 27

Month: August
Lucky Dates: 5, 7, 10, 14
Unlucky Dates: 2, 13, 27, 31

Month: September
Lucky Dates: 6, 10, 13, 18, 30
Unlucky Dates: 13, 16, 18

Month: October
Lucky Dates: 13, 16, 25, 31
Unlucky Dates: 3, 9, 27

Month: November
Lucky Dates: 1, 13, 23, 30
Unlucky Dates: 6, 25

Month: December
Lucky Dates: 10, 20, 29
Unlucky Dates: 15, 26

Days, Planets, Colors, and Goals

Day: Sunday
Planet: Sun
Correspondence: Exorcism, healing, prosperity
Color: Orange, white, yellow
Incense: Lemon, frankincense

Day: Monday
Planet: Moon
Correspondence: Agriculture, animals, female fertility, messages, reconciliation, voyages
Color: Silver, white, gray
Incense: African violet, honeysuckle, myrtle, willow, wormwood

Day: Tuesday
Planet: Mars
Correspondence: Courage, physical strength, revenge, military honors, surgery, breaking negative spells
Color: Red, orange
Incense: Dragon's blood, patchouli

Day: Wednesday
Planet: Mercury
Correspondence: Knowledge, communication, divination, writing, business transactions
Color: Yellow, gray, violet, all opalescent hues
Incense: Jasmine, lavender, sweet pea

Day: Thursday
Planet: Jupiter
Correspondence: Luck, health, happiness, legal matters, male fertility, treasure, wealth, employment
Color: Purple, indigo
Incense: Cinnamon, musk, nutmeg, sage

Day: Friday
Planet: Venus
Correspondence: Love, romance, marriage, sexual matters, physical beauty, friendships, partnerships
Color: Pink, green, aqua, chartreuse

Incense: Strawberry, rose, sandalwood, saffron, vanilla

Day: Saturday
Planet: Saturn
Correspondence: Spirit, communication, meditation, psychic attack or defense, locating lost or missing persons
Color: Black, gray, indigo
Incense: Poppy seeds, myrrh

Sun Sign Correspondences

Birth Date: March 21 to April 19
Sun Sign: Aries
Lucky and Protective Stones and Minerals: Diamond, amethyst, topaz, garnet, iron, steel
Color: Red

Birth Date: April 19 to May 20
Sun Sign: Taurus
Lucky and Protective Stones and Minerals: Coral, sapphire, emerald, turquoise, agate, zircon, copper
Color: Azure

Birth Date: May 20 to June 21
Sun Sign: Gemini
Lucky and Protective Stones and Minerals: Aquamarine, agate, amber, emerald, topaz, aluminum
Color: Electric blue

Birth Date: June 21 to July 22
Sun Sign: Cancer
Lucky and Protective Stones and Minerals: Opal, pearl, emerald, moonstone, silver
Color: Pearl, rose

Birth Date: July 22 to August 22
Sun Sign: Leo
Lucky and Protective Stones and Minerals: Diamond, ruby, gold, sardonyx, chrysoberyl
Color: Orange

Birth Date: August 22 to September 23
Sun Sign: Virgo
Lucky and Protective Stones and Minerals: Jade, rhodonite, sapphire, carnelian, aluminum
Color: Gray blue

Birth Date: September 23 to October 23
Sun Sign: Libra
Lucky and Protective Stones and Minerals: Opal, sapphire, jade, quartz, turquoise, copper
Color: Pale orange

Birth Date: October 23 to November 22
Sun Sign: Scorpio
Lucky and Protective Stones and Minerals: Bloodstone, topaz, aquamarine, jasper, silver
Color: Dark red

Birth Date: November 22 to December 21
Sun Sign: Sagittarius
Lucky and Protective Stones and Minerals: Lapis lazuli, topaz, turquoise, coral, tin
Color: Purple

Birth Date: December 21 to January 20
Sun Sign: Capricorn
Lucky and Protective Stones and Minerals: Onyx, jet,

ruby, lead, malachite
Color: Brown

Birth Date: January 20 to February 19
Sun Sign: Aquarius
Lucky and Protective Stones and Minerals: Aquamarine, jade, fluorite, sapphire, zircon, aluminum
Color: Green

Birth Date: February 19 to March 21
Sun Sign: Pisces
Lucky and Protective Stones and Minerals: Amethyst, alexandrite, bloodstone, stitchite, silver
Color: Ocean blue

Numbers

The following is based on the ancient Pythagorean system (on which modern-day numerology is based). If any number keeps appearing to you in various forms, pay attention to the meanings for that number.

One: Independence, new beginnings, self-development, oneness with life, individuality, progress and creativity

Two: A balance of yin and yang energies (the polarities) of the universe, self-surrender, putting others first, a dynamic attraction to one another, knowledge that comes from balancing the two opposites

Three: Trinity, mind-body-spirit, threefold nature of divinity, expansion, expression, communication, fun, self-expression, giving outwardly, openness and optimism (this number related to the Wiccan 3-by-3 law—whatever you send out, you will receive threefold)

Four: Security, foundations, four elements and the four directions, self-discipline through work and service, productivity, organization, wholeness

Five: Feeling free, self-emancipation, active, physical, impulsive, energetic, changing, adventuresome, resourceful, travel, curiosity, free soul, excitement, and change

Six: Self-harmony, compassion, love, service, social responsibility, beauty, the arts, generosity, concern, caring, children, balance, community service

Seven: Inner life and inner wisdom, seven chakras and seven heavens, birth and rebirth, religious strength, sacred vows, path of solitude, analysis, contemplation

Eight: Infinity, material prosperity, self-power, abundance, cosmic consciousness, reward, authority, leadership

Nine: Humanitarianism, selflessness, dedication of your life to others, completion, endings, universal compassion, tolerance, and wisdom

Master Numbers

In the Pythagorean tradition, master numbers were thought to have a special power and significance of their own.

Eleven: Developing intuition, clairvoyance, spiritual healing, other metaphysical faculties

Twenty-two: Unlimited potential of mastery in any area —spiritual, physical, emotional, and mental

Thirty-Three: All things are possible

A Full Moon By Any Other Name

Many of our full moon names come from medieval books of hours and also from North American Native Americana. Here are other, rarer names from these two traditions that you may want to use in your lunar rituals.

January: Old Moon, Chaste Moon
February: Hunger Moon
March: Crust Moon, Sugar Moon, Sap Moon, or Worm Moon
April: Sprouting Grass Moon, Egg Moon, Fish Moon
May: Milk Moon, Corn Planting Moon, Dyad Moon
June: Hot Moon, Rose Moon
July: Buck Moon, Hay Moon
August: Barley Moon, Wyrt Moon, Sturgeon Moon
September: Green Corn Moon, Wine Moon
October: Dying Grass Moon, Travel Moon, Blood Moon, Moon of Changing Seasons
November: Frost Moon, Snow Moon
December: Cold Moon, Oak Moon

Magical Intentions

The following words correspond to various planets and elements. See below to learn more.

Banishing: Saturn, fire
Beauty: Venus, water

Courage: Mars, fire

Divination: Mercury, air

Employment: Sun, Jupiter

Energy: Sun, Mars, fire

Exorcism: Sun, fire

Fertility: Moon, planet Earth

Friendship: Venus, water

Happiness: Venus, Moon, water

Healing and Health: Moon, Mars (to burn away disease), fire (the same), water

Home: Saturn, Earth, water

Joy and Happiness: Venus, water

Love: Venus, water

Money and Wealth: Jupiter, Earth

Peace: Moon, Venus

Power: Sun, Mars, fire

Protection: Sun, Mars, fire

Psychism: Moon, water

Sex: Mars, Venus, fire

Sleep: Moon, water

Spirituality: Sun, Moon

Success: Sun, fire

Travel: Mercury

Wisdom and Intelligence: Mercury, air

about the author

Cerridwen Greenleaf has worked with many of the leading lights of the spirituality world including Starhawk, Z Budapest, John Michael Greer, Christopher Penczak, Raymond Buckland, Luisah Teish, and many more. She gives herbal workshops throughout North America. Greenleaf's graduate work in medieval studies has given her the deep knowledge she utilizes in her work, making her work unique in the field. Her books have sold over 200,000 copies and received many awards.

Make sure to check out her inspiring blog

http://yourmagicalhome.blogspot.com/

also by
cerridwen greenleaf

The Witch's Book of Love Spells **ISBN-13** : 9781684811168

The Herbal Healing Handbook: **ISBN-13** : 9781633537149